AMERICA

An Illustrated Diary of Its of Its Most Exciting Years

POLITICS AND POLITICIANS

BOOK TWO

PRESS

A division of American Family Enterprises, Inc.

Robert Schramke—Publisher
Alan C. Hahn—Marketing Director
Robert Whiteman—Editorial Consultant
Marilyn Appleberg—Managing Editor
Louis Fulgoni—Book Design
Susan McQuibben—Picture Research

The Stonehouse Press—Production Supervision

PICTURE CREDITS

Bettmann Archive 61, 97; CBS 11, 117, 135; Culver 59, 61, 95; Library of Congress 80; National Archive 51, 53, 112; Sovfoto 20, 21, 26; UPI 13, 15, 17, 28, 32, 35, 36, 40, 41, 43, 45, 54, 61, 62, 64, 76, 77, 78, 83, 85, 87, 90, 91, 92, 93, 101, 105, 107, 113, 115, 119, 120, 121, 122, 140; US Army Photograph 23, 25, 48, 75, 109, 114, 138, 139, 140, 141. Wide World of Photo 11, 16, 29, 34, 49, 62, 67, 69, 71, 73, 99, 123, 127, 128, 130, 134, 139; Endleaves: Bettmann Archive, Brown Bros., Cinemabilia, Culver Pictures, Frederick Lewis, Granger Collection, Movie Star News, Library of Congress, UPI. Art: Robert Weaver 22, 47, 55, 65, 88-89, 103, 110, 125, 134-135, 137.

Printed in the United States of America

234567899 87654321

Table of Contents

POLITICS AND POLITICIANS

INTRODUCTION

On September 1, 1939, Hitler marched into Poland, and the Second World War was on. The "dress rehearsals"—Manchuria, Ethiopia, and Spain—were over. Before the "main event" ended in 1945, most of the world was to be involved.

New figures were to emerge on the world stage and many old ones would take new roles. Winston Churchill, Joseph Stalin, Chiang Kai-shek, Charles de Gaulle had starring parts. Towering above them was Franklin D. Roosevelt, who dominated world politics of the period until his sudden death in 1944.

At home, other names were appearing in the headlines: Wendell Willkie, Harry S. Truman, Thomas E. Dewey, Adlai Stevenson, Senators Arthur Vandenberg and Robert Taft, John L. Lewis.

On December 7, 1941, Japan attacked Pearl Harbor, and the isolationists were silenced. Headlines now featured Generals George C. Marshall, Dwight D. Eisenhower, Douglas Mac-Arthur, Admirals Chester Nimitz and William F. Halsey.

New words and place names appeared in the language after 1939: blitzkrieg, Maginot Line, underground, Dunkirk, the Coral Sea, the soft underbelly of Europe, D–Day, Iwo Jima, gas rationing, blackouts, Hiroshima, V–E and V–J Days.

After the shooting stopped, the United Nations came into being. Before too long, the U.N. was involved in Korea, and whether it was a war or a "police action," battles were fought and casualties—military and civilian—rose. Putting World War II hero General Douglas MacArthur in charge of U.N. forces led to a showdown between him and President Truman. Meanwhile, at the Capitol, America was going through the trauma of the McCarthy years.

Emerging as a political figure in the early 1950s was General Dwight D. Eisenhower, who was elected to two terms as President, retiring in 1960. America had faced many crises during the years between 1939 and 1960, and "Ike" had been close to most of them, as soldier or as President. Now, as America entered the 1960s, a whole new set of problems was waiting.

Mr. Roosevelt and the Third Term Dictatorship

by Senator Arthur H. Vandenberg

In October 1939, Senator Arthur H. Vandenberg of Michigan, an influential Republican, spoke out strongly against a Presidential third term.

One term? Two terms? Three terms?

How long should a President sit in the White House?

That is a burning question these days—and the chief reason it burns so hotly at the moment is the cryptic silence of one Franklin Delano Roosevelt regarding his intentions. One hundred and fifty years ago the world was full of kings—and we didn't like 'em. Today the world is full of dictators—and we don't like 'em. So we simply run true to form when we are critical of self-perpetuating Chief Executives. They just don't fit our pattern of democracy—and democracy is particularly sensitive to its hazards in this era of personal government all round the globe, not excluding Washington, D. C.

So the folks are talking it over and disagreeing on the subject—just as they talked and disagreed in the Constitutional Convention, just as they have talked and disagreed periodically in the story of the nation whenever an extended lease on 1600 Pennsylvania Avenue has been proposed. But thus far they have never concluded that any one man is more indispensable to the Republic than was George Washington when he was fathering his country.

Once renewed, however, the debate never stops with a clinic which is content to take apart the particular ego of the moment. It promptly leaps from the specific to the general theme—from the contemporary "man on horseback" to all men and all horses—and it always periodically proposes to save future generations from recurrent menace with "a law" which shall stop all future Caesars from even flirting with an American crown, or its equivalent.

With Nazism and Fascism to the right of us, and Communism to the left, and with "government by Executive decree" in possession of our own Capitol, it is small wonder that the present generation plunges into the debate with poignant avidity. Yes; and it ought to "plunge," because the White House tenure is inseverably linked with the maintenance of our republican institutions.

If a President, with all his normal power, ever gets the extraordinary power which will attach to him when he has once successfully crossed the traditional barrier against a third term, a fourth term and a fifth, and more, will be progressively and relatively simple achievements. The imperial state of mind which leads him to attribute indispensability to himself at the third hurdle will fatten to a conviction as to his own divinity at the fourth and fifth. Meanwhile his royal retinue—each knowing exactly what he wants—will beat the drums. But they will be the drums of doom for American democracy; because a perpetuated President, no matter how nobly meditated his imperial self-sacrifice, will be a despot in the making.

Despot In Making

And you can't blame the despot. Any time 130,000,000 people tell one mortal man that they can no longer find another among the remaining 129,999,999 to carry on the American system in the American tradition, it is *their* fault and not *his* if his delusions of grandeur transport him to Olympus.

Millions of Americans who immensely like the dynamic, magnetic F. D. R. would not vote him a third term in the White House—not because they love him less but because they love traditional American institutions and the spirit of democracy more. He is the last man who should be the one to break the third-term tradi-

Franklin D. Roosevelt, on the way to his first term as President, at 1932 Democratic National Convention.

Roosevelt delivers his inaugural address.

tion—if it is ever broken—because he is already the nearest personification of *personal government* in the United States that we have ever had in peace or war. He is a superlatively powerful personal character. He is a ruthless disciplinarian in matters of loyalty to his personal programs. I venture the assertion that his state papers contain more personal pronouns than any six of his predecessors' combined, not even excepting his illustrious predecessor of the same name. He believes in Executive dominion—as frankly confessed by his campaigns to tie courts and legislatures to his chariot wheel. He is intolerant of opposition. He believes in his own star of destiny. His judgments are pronounced with autocratic finality. Were he the greatest President we have ever had—which his satellites will freely concede—still he would supremely personify as no other could what the Senate had in mind when it adopted the La Follette resolution in 1928 by a vote of 56 to 26, and said:

"It is the sense of the Senate that the precedent established by Washington and other Presidents in retiring from the Presidential office after their second term has become, by universal concurrence, a part of our republican system of government, and that any departure from this time-honored custom would be unwise, unpatriotic, and fraught with peril to our free institutions."

Well—if that stricture could apply to a gentle, peaceful, unambitious Coolidge, what language could be mustered to fit the suggestion of a third term for his complete antithesis in the midst of "bread and circuses," who has himself bluntly asserted that he has "created instrumentalities of power" which, in what he conceives to be wrong hands, would "shackle the liberties of the people"? If it was "unwise, unpatriotic, and fraught with peril to our free institutions" for the safe and silent and conservative Coolidge to extend his Presidential term in a time which knew little of the psychology of dictatorship, what anathema could freedom conjure to describe the challenge to the present tumultuous hour?

Mind you, we are not now discussing the quality of Mr. Roosevelt's two administrations —we are discussing a system of government: the republican institutions of democracy of which a limited Presidency—limited by the voluntary fidelities of a century and a half of American tradition—is the supreme symbol, if not the supreme necessity.

Noisy Camp Followers

Mind you, too, I am not arguing with the President. I expect his patriotism to agree with these contentions. I am arguing, if at all, with those of his noisy camp followers who persistently call him to a third term—sometimes even embracing the amazing sophistry of pretending that it would only be his first term if he were re-elected in 1940, because he was robbed of his 1933-36 authority by a recalcitrant Supreme Court (which he has subsequently peopled with "sympathetic souls"), and robbed of his 1936-40 authority by a party rebellion (which increases its record for larceny the nearer we get to the next great showdown).

Silly? Yes. But could anything more clearly demonstrate the danger of such infatuations? Is it any wonder that most analytical Americans gratefully cherish the precedent set by George Washington and underwritten by Thomas Jefferson (whom today's New Dealers love to embrace as their progenitor) when he said in a letter to a friend:

"If some termination to the services of the Chief Magistrate be not fixed by the Constitution, or supplied by practice, his office, nominally for years, will in fact become for life; and history shows how easily that degenerates into an inheritance. Believing that a representative government responsible at short periods of election is that which produces the greatest sum of happiness to mankind, I feel it a duty to do no act which shall essentially impair that principle; and I should unwillingly be the first person who . . . should furnish the first example of prolongation beyond the second term of office."

It would be more in keeping with Jeffersonian doctrine than are most of the other innovations which have been clamped upon the country during the last few years in his great name if next winter's annual Jeffersonian dinners (which replenish contemporary political coffers at $100 a plate) should paint a slogan on their walls recalling the words of Jefferson's party, in response to their first President's self-renunciation, acclaiming "the manly and sublime effort which dictated your determination," and significantly deriving "consolation from the consideration that your example may operate on all future Presidents to pursue a course which has added luster to your character, already dear to liberty and your country."

I respectfully suggest to the distinguished President of the United States that nothing would be more fitting or more thrilling than that he should take advantage of next winter's Jefferson dinners to announce his own allegiance to this doctrine. Or the Jackson Day dinners (also used for contemporary fiscal rehabilitation) would be equally appropriate, because Old Hickory (another claimed New Deal ancestor) asked in each of his eight annual messages that Presidents be Constitutionally limited to *one* term.

Lest my suggestion be misconstrued by Charley Michaelson, the President's inimitably agile publicity director—who recently said that "It would clarify the present political situation if anybody could tell whether the G. O. P., its allies and affiliates, were more scared that the President *would* run for a third term than that he would *not* run," I must add parenthetically for myself, that I think he would be the most vulnerable nominee, as a third-term nominee, whom "the G. O. P., its allies and affiliates" could confront.

This problem is something infinitely more vital than whether somebody is "scared" or not. It goes to the roots of American institutions. From a purely political standpoint, many of us would confidently welcome the President's renomination for a third term as most clearly personifying the issues which the country must settle at the November polls in 1940. But from the standpoint of American institutional values, it would be happier to have the issue voluntarily settled in advance by the eloquent action of a great and powerful President himself. At any rate, I have the complete conviction that it will be settled—by whichever process in favor of the Washington-Jefferson precedent—which has been impregnable for one hundred and fifty years. The spirit of democracy is not yet ready for a rendezvous with disintegration.

Republican Senator Vandenberg spoke out against a third term for F.D.R.

13

But we were saying that each time this third-term issue arises the debate always resurrects the age-old contentions about limiting the Presidential tenure by Constitutional amendment. Some earnest souls proposed a limitation at one term of seven years. Others propose a general limitation to two terms; others, one term of six years, as recently suggested in a split report of the Senate Judiciary Committee.

Pre-Pledged One Term

Then there is a further suggestion, applicable to the immediate 1940 prospectus, which I submitted to my fellow countrymen in a statement last May and which would pre-pledge the next Republican nominee to one four-year term. It has nothing to do with any Constitutional change. No Constitutional change could possibly become effective, even in the doubtful event that one could be agreed upon, in time to control the President who will be inaugurated in January, 1941. Whatever happens in respect to the *next* President's tenure will still have to happen voluntarily (as is the theory of the existing Constitution). Obviously this suggestion has nothing to do with Mr. Roosevelt's tenure except as it is predicated upon his retirement or defeat.

I want to discuss this suggestion for a moment. I do not presume to infer that it deserves to be bracketed with other illustrious comments which I have been quoting. But perhaps it merits attention because I have received 3,912 separate newspaper editorials, pro and con (80 per cent pro), upon it.

On May 26, in a discussion of the next Republican Presidential nomination, I said this:

"The next Republican national convention must first set down cleancut, constructive, courageous principles which dependably promise to save the American system of free enterprise under the renewed spirit of Constitutional democracy, and to recapture prosperity for our whole people under a government restored to solvency. Then it should fit its nominations to its principles. It must strive to create common ground upon which all like thinkers may unite to produce an administration for all Americans in which a *pre-pledged one-term President* is manifestly free of all incentive but the one job of saving America."

It's the tenure which is important to this thesis. *One pre-pledged term!*

Why? Because if a Republican President should be elected in 1940, he will not have been elected merely by Republican votes. There is a sector of voters in this country—sufficient to dominate the 1940 outcome—which does not care a fig what *party* wins, so long as *America* wins. It was a *solidified opposition* to the Roosevelt party, regardless of previous partisan affiliations, which gave Republicanism its great stimulus last November. It will be a *solidified opposition* which will carry it to victory, if at all, in November, 1940. Like Lincoln's triumph in 1864, it will be a *coalition* victory utilizing the machinery of the Republican Party. It will demand a subsequent administration in kindred spirit—which is to say, an *all-American* administration "manifestly free of all incentive but the one job of saving America." The surest warrant for this outcome will be a *pre-pledged one-term President* (who means what he says) who can face the hard decisions which are the price of our emancipation not only without the hampering hobbles of political self-preservation to hold him back, but also without the sinister and destructive suspicions of his needed allies that they are helping to perpetuate a partisan dynasty.

Now let's get back to the abstract question of the Presidential tenure. Here are the two antithetical extremes: on the one hand, three terms for Roosevelt; on the other hand, one term of four years for his successor. In between lie the other possibilities—perhaps two four-year terms, as is the orthodox routine for acceptable Presidents; perhaps a Constitutional amendment determining once and for all upon one six-year term.

But, in spite of my deep conviction that no circumstance yet confronted in American experience could justify a third four-year term for any President, I want to say for myself that I doubt the wisdom of attempting to change the tenure or to limit it by Constitutional amendment. I think these decisions should be left to the patriotic and vigilant American conscience.

Who shall say that a tradition and a habit against a prolonged Presidency on the one hand, or freedom of action in behalf of a shorter prepledged Presidency on the other hand, is not better and safer than a Constitu-

14

tional stricture which could not be changed to fit one emergency or the other? The one is elastic under pressure of necessity; the other is a self-made barrier—erected by the people —against themselves—which is as insurmountable as, in some crises, it might be fatal.

In the presence of 1940, the people are free to elect Mr. Roosevelt for a third term if they wish. They are equally free to choose a pre-pledged one-term successor to him—or an unpledged two-term successor—if they wish. And since this is *their* government, it is illogical to tie their freedom of action. The very fact that proposed Constitutional strictures of one sort and another have always excited violent differences of opinion, and have always failed to jell, is the best possible proof that there never could be permanent assurance that any one particular Constitutional stricture would fit the changing vicissitudes of time and popular opinion.

Thus far it has always been perfectly safe to leave the decision to the people. So far as the third-term menace is concerned, it probably loomed largest in the person of President Grant. This produced the famous Springer resolution of 1875 in the House of Representatives, when the House, by the overwhelming vote of 234 to 18, resolved that no third term was a fundamental rule of the unwritten law of the Republic. Incidentally, it is significant to note that Grant was succeeded by a *pre-pledged one-termer*, President Hayes.

Eight Presidents have held office for two full terms. Two (Lincoln and McKinley) were elected to two terms but were cut down by

Franklin and Eleanor Roosevelt greet England's King George (far left) and Queen Elizabeth (far right) at Union Station, 1939.

Roosevelt broadcasts his final appeal to the voters from Hyde Park on the eve of the 1936 election.

assassination. Two (Theodore Roosevelt and Coolidge) passed from second to first place and served out full terms subsequently. Of the fourteen Presidents who completed a single term, only three (Polk, Buchanan, and Hayes) really made no effort to succeed themselves.

Theodore Roosevelt, when first assuming the Presidency, felt the anti-third-term tradition so keenly that he counted the three and one half years of his succession to the martyred McKinley as a full term and said: "The wise custom which limits the President to two terms regards the substance, and not the form, and under no circumstances will I be a candidate for, or accept, another nomination." In 1912, after four years' absence from the White House, he altered his doctrine to the extent of saying that the anti-third-term tradition runs against three *consecutive* terms. He ran again as a *non-consecutive* third-termer, and was defeated. If he had lived until 1920, he would probably have been renominated and he would probably have been elected as a *non-consecutive* third-termer. Thus the tradition would have been slightly bent if not actually broken. But the fact remains that it wasn't. The disturbing fact also remains that the second Roosevelt likes nothing better than to try to out-Roosevelt the first Roosevelt.

Well, there you are. We have had great varieties of Presidential tenure—thanks to Constitutional freedom in respect to it. I think it is probably wisest that both the freedom and the variety should continue. No one can conclusively say precisely how long any one citizen should claim the White House for his home. When Lincoln was asked how long a man's legs ought to be, he replied, "Long enough to reach the ground." That's the safest sort of answer to the question how long the President tenure ought to be. It ought to be long enough —or short enough—to fit the necessities of the contemporary moment.

We may safely leave the decision to the wisdom of the American people. That has been spectacularly true for one hundred and fifty years. It will still be true in 1940. I have my own ideas what they will say. They may choose a new President, Republican or Democrat, who is a first-termer without restrictive commitment for the future. They may choose a prepledged one-termer because of the immediate exigency. But they will not choose a third-termer at this particular moment when an upset world finds personal dictators at the throat of democracy and individual liberty all round the globe. They will not hazard an American paraphrase of this tragedy. And one reason they won't is that they probably will not have the chance. Any other eventuality would be "unwise, unpatriotic, and fraught with peril to our free institutions."

F.D.R. with Col. E.M. House, former advisor to President Wilson and Democratic kingmaker.

17

Hitler and Stalin—How Long Will It Last?

by Leon Trotsky

In early 1940, the year in which he was assassinated in Mexico by a Stalinist agent, Leon Trotsky wrote the following article.

When Hitler invaded Poland with lightning speed from the west, Stalin cautiously crept into Poland from the east. When Hitler, having subjected 23,000,000 Poles, proposed to end the "useless" war, Stalin through his diplomatic channels and his Comintern praised the advantages of peace. When Stalin occupied strategic positions in the Baltic, Hitler readily transferred his Germans elsewhere. When Stalin attacked Finland, Hitler's press, alone in the world, proclaimed its own complete solidarity with the Kremlin. The orbits of Stalin and Hitler are bound together by some internal attraction. What kind of attraction? How long will it last?

Twin stars are "optical"—that is, apparent; or "physical"—that is, true twins, forming a pair in which one star revolves about the other. Do Hitler and Stalin represent true or apparent twin stars in the present bloody sky of world politics? And if they are true twins, who revolves about whom?

Hitler himself speaks reservedly about the durable, "realistic" pact. Stalin prefers to smoke his pipe in silence. The politicians and journalists of the hostile camp represent Stalin as the main star and Hitler as the satellite in order to foment a quarrel between them. Let us attempt to analyze this by no means simple question, not forgetting that the orbits of world politics cannot be determined with such precision as the orbits of celestial bodies.

Objective: Redivide World

Having arisen much later than the western Powers, capitalist Germany constructed the most advanced and dynamic industry on the European continent; but it had been passed by in the previous division of the world. "We will divide it again," proclaimed the German imperialists in 1914. They were mistaken. The aristocracy of the world united against them and triumphed. Now Hitler hungers to repeat the experiment of 1914 on a more grandiose scale. He cannot help hungering for this. German capitalism is suffocating within the confines of her boundaries. Nevertheless Hitler's problem is insoluble. Even if he wins the war, the redivision of the world in favor of Germany cannot take place. Germany came too late. Capitalism is stifling everywhere. The colonies don't want to be colonies. The new World War will give a tremendous invigorated impulse to the movement for independence among the oppressed nations.

Hitler switches "friendships," evaluations of nations and governments, breaks agreements and alliances, dupes enemies and friends; but all this is dictated by one sole objective: redivision of the world. "Germany is not a world power at the present time," Hitler wrote in his book. But "Germany will become a world power or cease to exist." To convert united Germany into a base for European domination; to convert united Europe into a base for the struggle for world domination, consequently for confining, weakening, and reducing America—this task remains unchanged for Hitler. This end is for him the justification for the totalitarian regime which suppressed the class contradictions inside the German nation with an iron hoop.

Completely contradictory features characterize the U. S. S. R. Czarist Russia left a heritage of misery and backwardness. The mission of the Soviet regime is not that of securing new areas for the productive forces but that of erecting productive forces for the old areas. The economic tasks of the U. S. S. R. do not necessitate the extension of her borders. The level of her productive forces forbids a major war. The offensive power of the U. S. S. R. is not considerable. Her defensive power consists, above all, in her vast spaces.

Last March, after many years of extravagant official boasting, Stalin for the first time spoke at the convention of the Russian Communist Party on the comparative productivity of labor in the U. S. S. R. and the West. This excursion into the sphere of world statistics was made in order to explain away the poverty in which the peoples of the U. S. S. R. still live. In order to catch up with Germany in the production of pig iron, the U. S. S. R. in relation to its population would have to produce 45,000,000 tons a year instead of the 15,000,000 of today; in order to catch up with the United States, it would be necessary to raise the yearly production of pig iron to 60,000,000 tons—that is, to quadruple it. The same is true, and even more unfavorably, of all the other industries. Stalin, in conclusion, expressed the hope that the Soviet Union would catch up with the advanced capitalist countries during the next ten to fifteen years. Naturally, this time limit is questionable. But the involvement of the U. S. S. R. in a major war before the end of this period would signify in any case a struggle with unequal weapons.

The subjective factor, not less important than the material, has changed in the last years sharply for the worse. The tendency toward Socialist equality proclaimed by the revolution has been stamped out and defamed. In the U. S. S. R. there are twelve to fifteen million privileged individuals who concentrate in their hands about one half of the national income, and who call this regime "Socialism." On the other hand there are approximately 160,000,000 people oppressed by the bureaucracy and caught in the grip of dire poverty.

Hitler Needs War

The relations of Hitler and Stalin to the war are completely contradictory. The totalitarian regime of Hitler arose out of the fear of the possessing classes of Germany before a Socialist revolution. Hitler was mandated by the owners to save their property from the menace of Bolshevism at any cost, and to open up a passageway to the world arena. Stalin's totalitarian regime arose out of the fear of the new caste of revolutionary parvenus before the strangled revolutionary people.

War is dangerous for both of them. But Hitler is unable to carry out his historical mission by any different means. A victorious offensive war would secure the economic future of German capitalism and, along with this, the National Socialist regime.

It is different with Stalin. He cannot wage an offensive war with any hope of victory. In case the U. S. S. R. enters the war, with its innumerable victims and privations, the whole fraud of the official regime, its outrages and violence, will inevitably provoke a profound reaction on the part of the people, who have already carried out three revolutions in this century. No one knows this better than Stalin. The fundamental thought of his foreign policy is to escape a major war.

Stalin engineered an alliance with Hitler, to the surprise of all the diplomatic routinists and pacifist simpletons, because the danger of a major war could come only from Hitler, and because, according to the Kremlin's evaluation, Germany is mightier than her possible enemies. The protracted conferences in Moscow with the military delegations of France and England last summer served not only as a camouflage for the negotiations with Hitler but also as direct spying for military information. The general staff of Moscow became convinced, evidently, that the Allies were ill prepared for a major war. The thoroughly militarized Germany is a formidable enemy; it is possible to buy her benevolences only by co-operating in her plans.

Stalin's decision was determined by this conclusion. The alliance with Hitler not only eliminated for the time being the danger of involving the U. S. S. R. in a major war but also opened up the possibility of gaining immediate strategic advantages. In the Far East, Stalin retreated again and again for a number of years in order to escape war; on the western border the circumstances were such that he was able to escape war by fleeing—forward; not through giving up old positions but through taking new ones.

Hitler Made Payment

The press of the Allies pictures the situation as if Hitler were Stalin's prisoner, and exaggerates the gains that Moscow made at the expense of Germany—half of Poland (according to population about one third), plus domi-

19

nation of the eastern coast of the Baltic Sea, plus an open door to the Balkans, etc. The advantages won by Moscow are undoubtedly considerable. But the final score has not yet been settled. Hitler started war on a world-wide scale. From this struggle Germany will either emerge master of Europe and all the European colonies, or will founder. To safeguard his eastern flank in such a war is a question of life or death for Hitler. He paid the Kremlin with provinces of the former Czarist empire. Is this payment too high?

The argument that Stalin duped Hitler with his invasion of Poland and his pressure on the Baltic countries is completely absurd. It is much more probable that Hitler himself inspired Stalin to occupy eastern Poland and to lay hands on the Baltic States. Inasmuch as National Socialism grew out of a crusade against the Soviet Union, Stalin naturally could not depend upon Hitler's word of honor. The negotiations were carried out in a "realistic" tone. "You are afraid of me?" Hitler asked Stalin. "Do you want guaranties? Take them yourself." And Stalin took them. To picture it as if the new western boundary of the U. S. S. R. were

a permanent barrier to Hitler's road eastward violates all proportion. Hitler solves his tasks by stages. On the order of the day now is the crushing of Great Britain. For the sake of this objective it is possible to sacrifice something. The march eastward presupposes a major war between Germany and the U. S. S. R. When the time comes for this war, the question as to what meridian the struggle will begin upon will have only secondary significance.

The attack upon Finland seems at first glance contrary to Stalin's dread of war. But the matter in reality is different. Beside the blueprints there is an objective logic in the situation. In order to escape the war, Stalin made an alliance with Hitler. In order to safeguard himself against Hitler, he occupied a series of bases on the Baltic coast. However, Finland's resistance threatened to reduce all these strategic advantages to zero and even to convert them into their opposite. Who will settle accounts with Moscow if Helsinki refuses? Stalin, having read off "A," is compelled to read "B." Then follow the other letters in the alphabet. Stalin seeking to escape a war does not mean that war will permit Stalin to escape.

Stalin's Red Guard on parade.

Germany obviously pushed Moscow against Finland. Each step Moscow takes westward brings closer the involvement of the Soviet Union in the war. If this objective were gained, the world situation would change considerably. The Near and Middle East would become the arena of the war. The question of India would arise at once. Hitler would breathe with relief and, in case of an unfavorable turn of events, gain the possibility of concluding peace at the expense of the Soviet Union. Moscow undoubtedly gnashed its teeth upon reading the friendly articles in the German press. But gnashing one's teeth is not a political factor. The pact remains in force.

The immediate advantages to Moscow in the pact are indisputable. So long as Germany is occupied on the western front, the Soviet Union feels much more free in the Far East. This doesn't mean that offensive operations will be launched there. It is true that the Japanese oligarchy is even less capable of waging a war than the one in Moscow. However, compelled to face the west, Moscow cannot have the slightest motive for expanding in Asia. Japan, for her part, must consider that she could expect a serious and even annihilating resistance from the U. S. S. R. Under these conditions Tokyo must prefer the program of her navy—an offensive not to the west but to the south, toward the Philippines, Dutch East Indies, Borneo, French Indo-China, British Burma.

An agreement between Moscow and Tokyo on this basis would constitute a symmetric supplement to the pact between Moscow and Berlin. The question as to how this would influence the situation of the United States does not enter into the scope of this article.

Referring to the lack of raw materials in Russia itself, the world press insists upon the insignificance of the economic help which Stalin can render Hitler. The question, however, is not so simple. The lack of raw materials in the U. S. S. R. has a relative, not an absolute character; the bureaucracy in its drive for a high tempo of industrial development cannot maintain a proper balance between different sections of the economy. If the tempo of growth in various sections of industry is lowered for a year or two from 15 per cent to

10 or 5 per cent, still more if industrial production is maintained at the level of the preceding year, a significant surplus of raw materials immediately appears. The absolute blockade of German foreign trade will, on the other hand, inevitably divert a considerable amount of German exports to Russia in exchange for Soviet raw materials.

Moreover, it must not be forgotten that the U. S. S. R. has stocked and is still stocking immense reserves of raw materials and foodstuffs for defensive military purposes. A significant part of these reserves represents a potential source of supplies for Germany. In addition to this, Moscow can turn over to Hitler gold, which in spite of all the efforts to establish a closed economy remains one of the important sinews of war. Finally, the friendly neutrality of Moscow extraordinarily facilitates Germany in exploiting the resources of the Baltic countries, Scandinavia, and the Balkans. "Together with Soviet Russia," not without foundation wrote the *Völkischer Beobachter*, Hitler's organ, on November 2, "we dominate the sources of raw materials and foodstuffs of the whole East."

Several months before the conclusion of the pact between Moscow and Berlin, London evaluated more soberly than now the importance of the economic assistance which the U. S. S. R. could give Hitler. A semiofficial investigation conducted by the Royal Institute of International Affairs on the "political and strategic interests of the United Kingdom" (the introduction is dated March, 1939) declares in relation to the possibility of a Soviet-German rapprochement: "The danger to Great Britain of such a combination might be very great. It is questionable," continues the collective author, "how far Great Britain could hope to reach a decisive victory in any struggle with Germany unless the German eastern frontier could be blockaded by land." This evaluation deserves the most careful attention. It would not be an exaggeration to state that the alliance with the U. S. S. R. diminishes the effectiveness of the blockade against Germany by at least 25 per cent and perhaps considerably more.

Material and Moral Support

To the material support it is necessary to add—if this word is in place—the moral support. Up to the end of August the Comintern demanded the liberation of Austria, Czechoslovakia, Albania, Abyssinia, and was silent about

Adolf Hitler: "Feuhrer" of the German Third Reich.

23

the British colonies. Now the Comintern is silent about Czechoslovakia, supports the division of Poland, but demands the liberation of India. The Moscow *Pravda* attacks the suppression of liberties in Canada but is silent about the bloody executions of Czechs by Hitler and the tortures of Polish Jews. All this means that the Kremlin still has a high appraisal of Germany's strength.

And the Kremlin is right. Germany happened to be, it is true, incapable of launching a "lightning" war against France and Great Britain—but not a single serious person believed in such a possibility. However, the international propaganda which tries to picture Hitler as a lunatic driven up a blind alley is extremely light-minded. Hitler is still far from that. Dynamic industry, technical genius, the spirit of discipline—all this is present; the formidable German military machine will yet reveal itself. At stake is the fate of the country and the regime. The Polish government and the Czechoslovakian semigovernment are now in France. Who knows whether the French government will not have to seek refuge in Great Britain, together with the Belgian, Dutch, Polish, and Czechoslovakian governments?

I do not believe for a moment, as I have stated, in the actual realization of Hitler's plans concerning a *Pax Germanica*—that is, world domination. German imperialism arrived too late; its military fury will end in a tremendous catastrophe. But before that catastrophe occurs many things will topple in Europe. Stalin doesn't want to be among them. Above all, he safeguards himself from breaking with Hitler too soon.

The press of the Allies searches for symptoms of "coolness" between the new friends and every day predicts a rupture. It is impossible, indeed, to deny that Molotov does not feel too happy in Ribbentrop's embrace. For several years all internal oppositionists in the U. S. S. R. were branded, hounded, and executed as agents of the Nazis. Having finished this work, Stalin joined Hitler in a close alliance. Throughout the entire country there are millions of people intimately connected with those who were executed or imprisoned in the concentration camps because of their alleged alliance with the Nazis, and these millions are now cautious but extremely effective agitators against Stalin.

To this it is necessary to add the covert complaints of the Comintern—the unfortunate foreign agents of the Kremlin do not feel at ease. Stalin is undoubtedly attempting to leave open the other possibility. Litvinov was unexpectedly present on the tribune of Lenin's mausoleum on November 7. In the parade, portraits of the secretary of the Comintern, Dimitrov, and the leader of the German Communists, Thaelmann, were carried.

All this, however, is the decorative side of politics, not its substance. Litvinov, as well as the demonstrative portraits, was necessary above all for satisfying the Soviet workers and the Comintern. Only indirectly Stalin thus lets the Allies know that under certain circumstances he can change horses. But only visionaries could imagine that a reversal of the Kremlin's foreign policy is on the order of the day. So long as Hitler remains strong—and he is very strong—Stalin will remain his satellite.

All this may be true, an attentive reader can say, but what about revolution? Doesn't the Kremlin reckon with its possibility, probability, even inevitability? And doesn't speculation on revolution reflect itself in Stalin's foreign policy? The objection is legitimate. Moscow is the last to doubt that a major war will provoke revolution. But war does not begin, it ends with revolution. Before revolution broke out in Germany in 1918, the German army had succeeded in delivering mortal blows against Czarism. In the same way, the present war can crush the Kremlin bureaucracy long before revolution breaks out in some capitalist country. Our evaluation of the Kremlin's foreign policy consequently preserves its force independently of the perspective of revolution.

World Revolution?

However, in order to orient oneself correctly in the future maneuvers of Moscow and in the evolution of its relations with Berlin, it is necessary to answer the question: Does the Kremlin propose to utilize the war in order to further world revolution, and if so, then how? On November 9 Stalin considered it necessary to reject in an extremely blunt fashion the supposition that he wishes "the war to be prolonged as long as possible until its participants are completely exhausted." In this case

Stalin spoke the truth. He does not at all wish a prolonged war, for two reasons: first, it would inevitably draw the U. S. S. R. into its vortex; second, it would inevitably provoke revolution in Europe. The Kremlin quite legitimately dreads both.

"The internal development of Russia," declare the investigators for London's Royal Institute, "is tending to throw up a 'bourgeoisie' of managers and officials who possess sufficient privileges to make them highly content with the *status quo*. . . . It is possible to regard the various purges as part of a process by which all who desire to change the present state of affairs are being rooted out. Such an interpretation lends color to the belief that the revolutionary period in Russia is over, and that henceforward her rulers will only seek to conserve the gains which the revolution has brought them."

This is really well said! Over two years ago I wrote in *Liberty:* "Hitler is fighting against the Franco-Soviet alliance because he wants a free hand for agreement with Moscow against Paris." At the time these words were interpreted as a prejudiced opinion. Events corroborated it.

Moscow realizes very well that war on a major scale will bring an era of immense political and social repercussions. If those in Moscow could seriously hope to control the revolutionary movement and subordinate it to their own interests, Stalin naturally would welcome it. But he understands that revolution is the antithesis of bureaucracy and that it mercilessly sweeps aside the privileged, conservative apparatus. What miserable defeats the bureaucratic clique of the Kremlin suffered in the Chinese revolution of 1925-27 and in the Spanish revolution of 1931-39! On the wave of a new revolution a new international organization would inevitably arise which would wipe out the Comintern and deal a mortal blow to the authority of the Soviet bureaucracy in its national entrenchment in the U. S. S. R.

USSR And Spanish Civil War

It is surprising how little the lessons of the Spanish events have been understood. Defending himself from Hitler and Mussolini, who strove to utilize the civil war in Spain in order to construct a bloc of four Powers against Bolshevism, Stalin set himself the task of proving to London and Paris that he was capable of eliminating proletarian revolution from Spain and Europe with much greater efficiency than Franco and his backers. Nobody

Berlin 1940: Hitler and Field Marshall Herman Goering greet cheering throngs from balcony of Reich Chancery.

25

strangled the Socialist movement in Spain more mercilessly than Stalin, in those days an archangel of pure democracy. Everything was put into motion: a frenzied campaign of lies and frame-ups, legal falsifications in the spirit of the Moscow trials, systematic assassination of revolutionary leaders. The struggle against the seizure of land and factories by the peasants and workers was conducted, naturally, under the name of the struggle against "Trotskyism."

The civil war in Spain deserves minutest attention, as in many respects it bore the aspects of a rehearsal of the incipient World War. In any event, Stalin is completely ready to repeat his Spanish performance on a world-wide scale, with the hope of better success this time in buying the friendly attitude of the future victors through having proved that no one better than he can curb the Red specter which for terminological convenience will again be labeled "Trotskyism."

For five years the Kremlin conducted a campaign in favor of an alliance among the democracies in order to sell to Hitler at the last moment their love for "collective security and peace." The functionaries of the Comintern received their order, "Left face," and immediately dug out of the archives old formulas about Socialist revolution. The new "revolutionary" zigzag will probably be shorter than the "democratic" one because wartimes accelerate the tempo of events enormously. But Stalin's fundamental tactical method remains the same: He converts the Comintern into a revolutionary menace to the enemies of tomorrow in order to exchange it at the decisive moment for a favorable diplomatic combination. There is not the slightest reason to fear resistance from the Browders or from people of his type.

A Bluff By Stalin?

Through its docile correspondents, the Kremlin threatens that in case Italy or Japan joins England and France, Russia will enter the war on Hitler's side, striving at the same time to sovietize Germany. (See, for example, the Moscow dispatch in the *New York Times*, November 12.) Astonishing confession! Through the chain of its "conquests" the Kremlin is already so tied to the chariot of German imperialism that the possible future enemies of Hitler automatically become enemies of Stalin. His probable participation in the war on the side of the Third Reich, Stalin promptly covers with a promise to "sovietize" Germany. After the pattern of Galicia? To accomplish this it would be necessary to occupy Germany with the Red army. By means of an insurrection of the German workers? But if the Kremlin enjoys this possibility, why does it wait for Italy and Japan to enter the war?

The motive of the inspired correspondence is too clear: to frighten on the one hand Italy and Japan, and on the other England and France—and thereby to escape the war. "Don't push me to extremes," Stalin threatens, "or I will commit terribles deeds." This is at least 95 per cent bluff and perhaps 5 per cent nebulous hope that in case of mortal danger revolution will bring salvation.

The idea of Stalin's sovietizing Germany is as absurd as Chamberlain's hope for the restoration of a peaceful conservative monarchy there. Only a new world coalition can crush the German army through a war of unheard-of proportions. The totalitarian regime can be crushed only by a tremendous attack on the part of the German workers. They will carry out their revolution, surely, not in order to replace Hitler with a Hohenzollern or Stalin.

The victory of the popular masses over the Nazi tyranny will be one of the greatest explosions in world history and will immediately change the face of Europe. The wave of awakening, hope, enthusiasm will not stop at the hermetic borders of the U. S. S. R. The popular masses of the Soviet Union hate the greedy and cruel ruling caste. Their hate is only dampened by the idea, Imperialism is watching us. Revolution in the west will deprive the Kremlin oligarchy of its sole right to political existence. If Stalin survives his ally Hitler, it will not be for long.

A military parade in Moscow, 1938.

What Kind of President Would Senator Taft Make?

by Frederick L. Collins

Senator Robert A. Taft, son of the twenty-seventh President and Chief Justice, was a serious candidate for the Republican nomination in 1940.

Bob Taft is the despair of the newsreel men. Before the camera he is willing, but the ham just isn't in him. Besides, his gift for the photographically inappropriate is monumental.

Every candidate for national office has to have his picture taken with a cow. No one seems to know why, but it is so. The campaign photograph of Mr. Taft with cow discloses ardent Farmer Taft, in white collar, dark street suit, light fall overcoat, and fedora hat, gingerly poking the animal's snout with neatly gloved hand.

Another shot shows Candidate Taft, a big outdoors man this time, hatless and gloveless but otherwise irreproachably garbed in blue serge business suit, holding at arm's length a wild turkey somebody else killed.

Caught unaware by the candid camera, the effect is equally bad. At work, he seems all spectacles. If they aren't on his nose, blotting out his gentle humorous eyes, they are hanging from his ear or stuck in his teeth. He hasn't swallowed them yet, but Mrs. Taft lives in daily fear.

Yet the real point of those seemingly incongruous and unfortunate pictures is simply that it never occurs to him to be "artificially natural" before a camera. He is always Bob Taft rather than Taft the hunter or Taft the farmer or anything else. He works his farm in overalls, but has never thought to step into them while posing with a cow. On that hunting trip, he had himself shot a deer and he had posed in his hunting togs with it. After changing to a business suit, he good-naturedly permitted a cameraman who had come late to take him with the turkey.

The man just isn't publicity-conscious. The Tafts celebrated their twenty-fifth anniversary last year, but the newspaper boys didn't hear about it for months afterward. It never occurred to Bob Taft that any one would be interested in his silver wedding anniversary except himself and Martha Taft.

Poor Speaker

Sometimes it seems that he isn't politics-conscious, either. Friendly as he has been to the A. F. of L., in Kansas City he blundered through an A. F. of L. picket line which had been in existence more than a year. In Des Moines, he chose the day Iowa farmers were getting $70,000,000 in new federal corn loan money to denounce, as a permanent policy, the New Deal's corn loan plan.

In addition to all of which, Bob Taft makes what most politicians consider a damned poor speech. They base their judgment on what they think the people want in the speech-making line. As for him, he plows right ahead. Poor speaker or not, he has stood up in debate against the most silver-tongued New Dealers, and has won decisions in the polls of popular opinion.

The man with the most delegates on the Republican side of the campaign for the Presidency is, at the present writing, this same Bob Taft. While others have been winning popularity contests, he has been winning delegates. He already has more than three hundred pledges to support him. No one else has a hundred.

All of which does not mean that Taft will be nominated on the first ballot. It may not mean that he will be nominated on the last. But it does mean, if we can judge by political conven-

27

tions in the past, that no one else can be until his supporters have talked business with Mr. Taft.

He wouldn't be the easiest man in the world with whom to talk about it. He knows what has happened before in boss-manipulated national conventions. Sometimes a deal is made. The Vice-Presidency is the usual bait to get a candidate in Bob Taft's strategic position to withdraw in favor of the man the bosses prefer. But Bob doesn't want the Vice-Presidency.

He has already made a strong bid for the Presidency—much stronger than most of us know. He has the best organization in the field, the best tactical position, the most votes.

His selection might be a flouting of the people's choice—and it might be its true expression—but Robert A. Taft, with a third of the Republican Convention already at his back, is a man to be reckoned with in this Presidential race. Politically, he is the man of the hour. Republicanly speaking, he may be the man of the year. It certainly behooves us all to know what kind of man he is.

Well, the first most of us outside of Ohio heard of Bob Taft was in 1934, when he sued the United States government for $1.07, and carried the Case to the United States Supreme Court.

We knew in a general way that Bob didn't sue because he needed the buck, even though he is essentially a self-made man. William H. Taft, the only man in his country's history to be both President of the United States and Chief Justice of the Supreme Court, was not a rich man; neither was he poor. He was known to have left an estate of almost half a million, but he left all of it to his widow and daughter, noting with pride that his sons were now able-bodied, educated men who could take care of themselves. Charles P. Taft, uncle of Bob and young Charlie, had married Annie Sinton, the richest girl in Cincinnati, had himself become wealthy, and was known to have left driblets of his estate to his nephew, Bob; most of it he had given away in philanthropies. But, as every Ohioan knew, the young man himself, by assiduous practice of estate and corporation law, had become what he modestly describes as "well-to-do."

The man must, therefore, be a crank or a citizen of profound convictions. An examina-

28

tion of the situation which caused him to bring this suit tipped the scales toward the second explanation.

When the United States fell off the gold standard, President Roosevelt suspended gold payments, and Congress, then completely under his spell, obediently voided all contracts to pay in gold, thus repudiating at a stroke the "gold clause" in approximately $100,000,000,000 worth of bonds.

Moral Issue

Robert Taft was one of many Americans who considered this repudiation of a definite promise to pay an immoral and illegal act. So he selected one bond as a test case, and went to court to recover the interest he had lost. The moral issue has never been decided. Court after court held that Congress had sole right to decide what should be used for money. Bob Taft kept on, nevertheless, until he got his final comeuppance from the Nine Old Men.

By this exhibition of tenacity and courage he won the admiration of those few citizens who, in 1933 and 1934, still had a few dollars; but on most of us his courageous stand against New Deal currency juggling made no lasting impression.

Robert A. Taft with a non-voting admirer.

When, therefore, Bob Taft next emerged into national spotlight in 1936 as Ohio's favorite son in the Republican Convention which nominated Landon, we still knew so little of him we concluded the papers must have meant brother Charlie.

Young Charles P. Taft, second son of William H. and inheritor of his father's chuckle and dimples, had won considerable fame for himself as leader of the movement for a city-manager form of government in Cincinnati, and had written an excellent book extolling this form. He was also a good-looking, popular, hail-fellow-well-met chap, active in religious and labor movements, a very plausible candidate for high office.

As for big brother Bob, some one has said that he looks like a composite picture of 16,000,000 Republicans. If he does, the composite Republican is tall and thin-haired, has a waist-line that is—er—comfortably expanded, a mouth that is too big for his face, and kindly, friendly gray-blue eyes behind spectacles.

He has a nice grin, which discloses rows of large protruding teeth. Add to all this a general sand-blond ineffectiveness as to eyebrows and wispy hair, a solemn, ponderous manner, and you have something right out of a Grant Wood portfolio.

The Tafts at their Canadian summer home.

"Plain Man"

"A big plain friendly man" is the way his wife describes him; and, of course, she is right. But the Ohio politicos might well have looked at him askance. His father, President Taft, for all his weight, was a handsome man, and a well dressed man, too. He owned all the right duds, and never rebelled at getting into them. Son Robert's dark gray or blue effect is known in the family as the "Taft all-purpose suit," and to get him out of it into anything more demanding than pajamas is a task which requires the forcible insistence of Mrs. Taft and of the Tafts' four strapping sons.

"When Bob was to take his seat in the Senate last year," relates Mrs. Taft, who looks amazingly like the present Queen of England, "I was thrown into great consternation by word from the senior senator, who was to introduce my husband, that a 'cutaway' would be proper attire for the occasion. Bob's cutaway dated from

his wedding, when he was twenty-four years younger and many inches slimmer. It took the combined efforts of the family to get him into it, and when he set off for the Capitol we were apprehensive that the seams might not stand the strain."

But Bob Taft fooled everybody, including his wife.

"What was our surprise," she continues, "when we looked down upon him from the gallery an hour later to see him in an easily fitting cutaway, obviously chuckling at our surprise. He had bought a new suit on his way to the Capitol, and all was well."

In retrospect, the Tafts got a lot of fun out of this incident; for the senior senator was none other than old Vic (Baked Potato) Donahey, who has made himself one of the greatest vote getters in Ohio history by stressing the fact that he comes from the "plain peepul," which he does, whereas Bob Taft has always been handicapped in his appeal for popular support by the wealth of his family and its social position!

The point at issue here, however, is that Bob has seldom bothered to embellish his unflashy exterior with the kind of clothes which sometimes make the man. Nor has he made a habit of kissing any babies except his own, and since these now range from fourteen to twenty-four, he is getting kind of out of practice even in his homework. As for backslapping and rib-poking and chin-chucking, they simply aren't in the man.

Genial Not Jovial

His father never went in much for baby kissing, either. He didn't need to. Bill Taft had many things about him, including the fact that he was a fat man, to make everybody love him. He liked to hear a good story, and told one well. The twinkles in his eyes, the dimples in his cheeks, even the rockings of his great body, drew men to him. His chuckle, born of a true joviality, filled the room.

Bob Taft has a sense of humor, but his expression of it, even in the inner circle of his friends, is genial rather than jovial. Among strangers or chance acquaintances, like most shy men, he assumes a dignity which often passes for austerity. He shrinks from meeting strangers because he really thinks that they wouldn't be interested in meeting him.

In the rough-and-tumble of campaigning, which he has come to enjoy, he has learned to turn on the smiles once in a while, even to indulge in a quiet quip or two. During his Senatorial campaign, at a stock sale in Belmont, Ohio, he auctioned off a calf for 14½ cents a pound. The previous high had been 9 cents. Whereupon he amazed his managers by saying, "It just shows what I can do with the farm problem if given half a chance."

In Washington, where he insists on driving his own car just as he did in Cincinnati, the Tafts were spotted one night as they came out of an official reception by a brass-buttoned flunky, who immediately shouted:

"Senator Taft's car!"

"Thank you," said Bob, touching the great man on the gold-braided sleeve. "It's a good car, but it doesn't come when it's called." Then he and Martha slipped off down the street to the parking place.

Many a good quality forth-right, hard-working Bob Taft was known by his intimates to possess; but even they were surprised when the news broke about his being chosen as Ohio's favorite son in 1936.

The circumstances of the choice were, on the surface, unfortunate. Nobody really knows yet whether the city-manager idea for municipalities is good or bad. But it has always worn the halo of reform. Machine politicians are usually against it, and individuals who oppose it are apt to be tarred with the machine stick. While Charlie was fighting for this supposedly righteous cause as one of the Charterite group in Cincinnati, Bob, who has always been a strict party man, stuck by the organization, feeling that he could accomplish more for good government by working within the existing Republican Party. His subsequent selection, therefore, as favorite son was viewed merely as a boss-given reward for that action, although he was later to fight the machine candidate in his Senate race.

Two years later this man nobody knew—that is, outside of Ohio—was entering the United States Senate and was being actively urged by national leaders as a candidate for President.

What had happened?

Plenty. In the first place, and least importantly, he had put up an unexpectedly good fight in the primaries against the late Senator Borah and had given him an unexpected licking. The result, however, did not shake the nation or even his own state.

Bob Taft was sort of taken for granted in the Buckeye State. The Taft family had long been a Cincinnati museum piece. Bob and Charlie had inherited responsibilities incumbent on heirs to a throne.

Intense Little Boy

Older Cincinnatians remembered Bob as an intense little blond boy sometimes crouched in adoration in old Fire House 10, listening to tales of prowess from the gallant firemen.

Family friends remembered how he had to give up caddying for his distinguished father because he bawled with mortification every time Papa Taft missed a putt—which was plenty often. They remembered, too, that when young Bob was old enough to take up the family game of chess, he bawled just as loudly with anger at himself, not because he had lost a game but because he had not won.

Came a time when Fire Company 10 saw him no more. Judge Taft had to go to the Philippines, of which McKinley had appointed him Civil Governor. The boys at the fire house gave Bob a complete set of fire signals to take with him to Manila. That fact is about all that the grown Bob seems to remember about his Far Eastern experiences—except that the Malacanan Palace, where the Governor General lived, was really a big house on stilts, and that he and Charlie used to go swimming off the porch in the dirty water below.

After a couple of years the boy was shipped home by army transport to begin his serious scholastic career at Uncle Horace Taft's famous school in Connecticut. He proceeded to lead his class at Taft, lead his class at Yale, lead his class at Harvard Law School.

"That's a rather overpowering record to his four sons," laughed Mrs. Taft. "They never hear about it from him, but are frequently and pointedly reminded of it by their mother."

The Tafts always had been good at their schoolbooks. Grandfather Alphonso had been third in his class at Yale; Father Bill, second in his. Bob simply had to keep up the progression and be first. He was also consumed at this period with a determination to be something on his own account and not just "Bill Taft's boy." His schoolbooks gave him that opportunity.

No Y

At his uncle's school he went out for the football team, but bad eyesight kept him off the first squad. As a jayvee, however, he showed that old desire to excel. One day the first-team tackle against whom Bob played in practice went to the coach to say:

"You'll have to do something about Taft. He tackles me every time just as if we were playing Hotchkiss."

At Yale, Bob got plenty of A's but no Y. However, he has had the satisfaction recently of having been singled out by Yale alumni to receive the Montclair-Yale Bowl, a trophy rewarded annually to a graduate who has made his Y in life.

By the time Bob got to college his father had

gotten to the White House, or, at least, was on his way. Bob's shyness made him want to keep mighty quiet about it.

All the Taft children were like that. Sister Helen Taft, on a shopping tour in New York while their residence was the White House, was asked by a salesgirl to give her father's name and address. "W. H. Taft," she replied. "He lives in Washington at 1600 Pennsylvania Avenue."

After law school, Bob, who had been scouted by practically every big Manhattan law firm, refused all offers, dashed back to his native Cincinnati, passed his bar exams—with the highest grade, of course, of any applicant in the state!—married Martha Bowers, gay, pretty brown-eyed daughter of his father's Solicitor General, Lloyd Bowers, went to work for an old established firm of counselors, and reported for duty at Republican precinct headquarters.

Decorated For His Work

When war came, he promptly enlisted, only to be turned down on two attempts because of those confounded nearsighted eyes. So he did the next best thing: enlisted under Hoover, became assistant counsel to the Food Administration and later counsel to the American Relief Administration in Europe. For his work abroad he was decorated by Poland, Finland, and Belgium—three excellent countries for a 1940 Presidential candidate!—but no one has ever seen him wearing the buttons.

Back in Cincinnati, he became precinct committeeman, a post which he still holds. He has since been chairman of the Republican Executive Committee of Hamilton County, and is now chairman of Columbia Township, the suburb where he lives.

Both Bob and Martha would disown that suburban implication. They consider themselves farmers, and, as a matter of fact, their home is on a sixty-acre farm which has been kept in cultivation every year. Martha takes charge of the flower garden, and Bob of the fruit and vegetable crops. A roadside stand is maintained to sell produce to passing motorists, just as on any other farm.

He was a member of the Ohio House of Representatives from 1921 to 1926, floor leader in '25, Speaker in '26; member of the Ohio Senate in '31-32. As chairman of a special Senate tax committee, he revolutionized a bad taxation situation affecting Ohio municipalities. By 1938 he was a well known figure in the state, but he had never been seriously considered by the leaders for the Big Time.

The bosses doubted the popular appeal of a man of his type. The Neil House crowd which rules Ohio Republican politics liked him well enough. Although not strictly one of them, he had, whenever his conscience would let him, co-operated in the forwarding of party measures. But as a potential vote getter they felt that he lacked "color." So, although it was well known that he wanted the 1938 nomination for the United States Senate, they chose instead Judge Arthur Day, who is the mixer type.

Bob and Martha talked it over.

A Stiff Proposition

It isn't too much to say that if shy and retiring Bob Taft goes to the White House, it will be primarily Martha's doing. Not that she has made him what he is today. But she has revealed him to the world and, perhaps, to himself.

When Martha Bowers first met Robert Taft, in the days when he was a Yale undergraduate and she was a Washington subdeb, Bob was a pretty stiff proposition. His shyness and his preoccupation with intellectual matters did not contribute to his possibilities as a ladies' man or, for that matter, as one of the boys.

It would have been easy for a popular, high-spirited girl like Martha Bowers to set down lanky Bob as whatever was the 1913 equivalent of "sourpuss" and let him go at that. Far from doing so, she began by inducing the gang to play charades—in which Bob did not shine as an actor but beat all comers at guessing the answers—and in time she worked him up to the point where he danced a very neat "Boston" and even went for jolly before-breakfast rides in Rock Creek Park.

Married to Taft in 1914, she became at once, with her beauty and her social tact, a tremendous political asset to the bashful and near-sighted young politician. "As each guest introduced himself," wrote an observer of one of the Tafts' earlier receptions, "Mrs. Taft grasped his hand firmly, looked him straight in the

In golf and politics "Bob doesn't shoot so far, but he stays on the course," said Martha Taft.

32

eyes, repeated his name, and started a conversation. Every hand she shook won a heart and a vote."

Bob himself is not a man easily discouraged. Martha is a feminine Rock of Gibraltar. So, after talking matters over in the summer of 1938, they decided that it didn't make any difference to them whether a lot of politicians wanted Bob for United States Senator. *They* wanted him. So they would go it alone.

Bob Beat Day

Bob drove his car thirty thousand miles, made over six hundred speeches. His wife very nearly equaled this record, not speaking so often as her husband, but evening up by attending innumerable receptions, teas, and sociables. Altogether, Martha Taft appeared in eighty-five of Ohio's eighty-eight counties.

Against this double threat Happy Day did the best he could. But the voters believed Bob and Martha. Taft beat Day by 62,000.

But beating the New Deal's baby, Senator Bulkley, in the election wouldn't be so easy, politicians said. Bulkley had factors working for him which were not present in the case of hapless Happy Day. Chief among these, of course, was the relief money which Republican Governor Bricker is *not* now getting for Ohio.

Besides, Bulkley stood on his record in the Senate, which, from a New Deal standpoint, was excellent. Finally, he had behind him the smooth-running, thoroughly Farleyized Democratic machine, which had acquired both speed and direction during six fat years of federal patronage.

But Bob Taft has a way of brushing aside considerations which lie outside the main issue of whether a course is right or wrong. He has held from the beginning of his conflict with the Roosevelt administration that the New Deal must be beaten "if the American system of individual enterprise and free government were to be maintained," and that it could be beaten if the issues were once clearly drawn.

The best way to get the issues squarely joined in this 1938 campaign was, he figured, to get Senator Bulkley, the acknowledged New Deal champion, on the same platform with him, and to fight it out as Lincoln and Douglas did. So, against the advice of all his advisers

except Martha, he challenged his opponent to a series of debates.

"Senator Bulkley accepted, and he is probably still wondering why," said Morris D. Ervin, Washington correspondent of the *Cincinnati Times-Star*, writing in the *Christian Science Monitor*. "The first debate was held in Marietta. . . . There was a good deal of cheering and booing. When Bulkley was booed he became angry. He stopped talking and waited for the booing to stop. . . . All that the radio audience could hear was the booing.

"When it came Taft's turn to talk, the other side began to boo him. But Taft didn't forget his radio audience. . . . He hugged the microphone and went right on talking. Result—the radio audience heard Taft and didn't hear the boos. Taft won over Buckley by 170,000 votes."

Active Debater

Once safely in the Senate, Taft went on ignoring political traditions, especially the one that baby senators should be seen and not heard. The junior senator from Ohio became one of the most active debaters on the floor; and the outstanding feature of every one of his speeches was, as always, clarity.

"The only way we are going to stop spending is to stop paying money out," he said in his first one; "and the surest way of preventing the paying out of money is not to appropriate the money to be paid out."

During the debate on the $3,000,000,000 spend-lend proposal, Taft, with his gift for figures, was a tower of strength to the Republican-Democratic coalition which wrecked the President's program.

One of the big radio systems conceived the idea of staging a debate between representatives of the New Deal and of the opposition. For the New Deal man the radio boys chose a practiced radio speaker, Congressman Thomas V. Smith, once a professor of philosophy at the University of Chicago. For the opposition they sought several outstanding Republican orators, who politely declined to swap wisecracks with glib Mr. Smith. Finally, they got down to Taft.

Against the advice of his friends, Bob accepted the challenge. When his friends offered to write his speeches, Bob said he wouldn't feel honest speaking somebody else's words. So he just gave them his own words. For example:

On government spending: "No nation has ever continued indefinitely an unbalanced budget without ultimate collapse."

On the NLRB: "No human being exists who can be completely impartial in deciding a case on which he has already taken a public position."

On unemployment: "Work relief and direct relief should be consolidated under local administration. The present overhead organization is top-heavy. Out of approximately $900 spent per case per year, the WPA workers get only about $600."

Sounds kind of commonsensical, doesn't it?

A 50-50 Chance

Evidently the listeners-in thought so. About three million people heard each one of the thirteen debates. A Gallup poll, taken at the conclusion of the thirteen-weeks period, showed 66 per cent for Taft, 34 per cent for Smith. The Mr. Smith who went to Washington took his defeat gracefully.

"If the country has to suffer a Republican President," he said, "my hope is that it will be Mr. Taft."

Has he a chance?

Well, the political wise men seem to think that he has at least a 50-50 Republican chance —not alone for the reasons which we have been considering here but because of elements in the situation itself.

For example, age may have a great deal to do with choosing the next President. The leading Republican candidate in the current polls is thirty-eight. The leading Democratic candidate—always excepting Mr. Roosevelt—is seventy-two. Voters have usually chosen Presidents whose ages lie in between these extremes. Bob Taft is fifty—not too old, not too young.

Geography is also frequently a deciding factor in the choice of Presidents. Politicians, especially Republican politicians, have a strong preference for candidates born near the center of the population. Seven of the last eleven Republican Presidents have come from Ohio, the pivotal state, the Taft state.

So it would seem that all the senator from Ohio has to do, so far as the nomination goes, is to keep his eye on the ball—and on his three hundred delegates—which he will undoubtedly do. For, as Martha says:

"Bob doesn't shoot so far, but he stays on the course!"

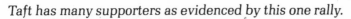

Taft has many supporters as evidenced by this one rally.

What Kind of President Would Willkie Make?

by Morris Markey

Wendell L. Willkie, a Hoosier industrialist new to politics, was the subject of a phenomenal popular boom in 1940.

He is the head of a billion-dollar corporation —a utilities corporation, at that. His office is just one block off Wall Street. Nobody knows for sure whether he is a Democrat or a Republican. And yet people are saying, in numbers which grow by thousands every day, "There's a man who would make a great President."

To increase the paradox, it isn't Wall Street saying that. Out over the country a sort of murmur can be heard among all sorts of people who are bewildered by the fight between the two great parties: "Wendell Willkie would make a wonderful President. But how in the world could he ever be elected?"

And down in Pine Street, Willkie sits with his feet on his desk, listening to his innumerable visitors and smiling with the curiously compelling smile which belongs to his remarkable personality.

He offers no encouragement to his well-wishers. He says with blunt finality that he will not lift a hand to get the nomination. And then he looks at the huge count of his daily mail. He fingers the invitations from colleges and societies and clubs to come and speak to them. (There were 1,200 of these on his desk in one day.) And he says, "No honest man could deny an interest in this propostion."

The Willkie boom is that rare bird in American politics, a movement which started literally of its own accord.

It all began with his fight against the New Deal over the Tennessee Valley Authority. His corporation, Commonwealth & Southern, served Tennessee with electric power—along with ten

"Stamford (Conn.) Welcomes Willkie" at the start of New England campaign tour, 1940. Below, Willkie's final Presidential campaign speech, Madison Square Garden.

other states. The New Deal built the vast power plants of TVA and told Willkie it would run him out of business by underselling him. Willkie did not mince words in his objection to the idea. He said that competition between government and private enterprise was vicious. And he demanded that if the government insisted upon going into business it should buy up his Tennessee properties at a fair price to the stockholders. He made the demand stick. He got his fair price.

Fight Out In Open

It was the way Willkie handled it that roused the interest of the ordinary man. Unlike most big shots of big business, he did not believe in working quietly behind the scenes, pulling a string here and a string there, using the immense resources of his company to overpower resistance. He took his fight into the open. He charged down on the New Deal with biting accusation, spoken with all of his uncommon vigor and eloquence.

In the midst of this fight the Presidential boom of Robert H. Jackson, the Attorney General, got under way. Beneath the halo of Roosevelt's approving smile, Jackson went out to show himself to the country in a series of broadcast speeches. His theme was always the same: a savage and unremitting attack upon business, and the utilities business in particular.

Willkie took up the challenge. He met Jackson in open debate in Town Hall, over a nationwide network.

The listeners of America heard Mr. Jackson get his ears pinned back that night. They heard the last of the Jackson boom. General Hugh Johnson, a great friend of Jackson, wrote that Willkie "made a perfect monkey of him."

People began to realize that here was something new under the American sun: a competent and successful business man who had never held a political office and who could outwit professional politicians in their own language, on their own battleground.

That was his first real public appearance. A second and somewhat less public appearance that he made a few weeks later was perhaps even more important.

At the Harvard Club, in New York, the brilliant Felix Frankfurter, New Dealer, now justice of the Supreme Court, spoke to a gathering of several hundred men. Following the address a discussion ensued. An informal debate sprang up between Willkie and Frankfurter, and for the next three hours the audience sat enthralled. For a business man to stand up and hold his own against the nimble-minded Frankfurter for so long was a sensation. And the several hundred men went out of that room to spread word that here was a new prophet of liberalism and democracy.

Within a week five publishers had asked him to write a book about the American way. And people who had never heard of him before began to ask, "Who is this Willkie? Where did he come from? What has he done?"

Who Is Willkie?

He was born forty-eight years ago in Elwood, Indiana. The liberal tradition was part of his birthright, because all four of his grandparents had fled from the heel of German despotism to America. The original family name was Willcke.

His father and mother were both lawyers, the latter being the first woman admitted to the Indiana bar. One of his grandmothers was a Presbyterian preacher, and one of his aunts a doctor.

His father became celebrated for his trial work and made a fortune at his practice. But the fortune was wiped out in the panic of '93, and thereafter Willkie Senior devoted all his energies to his one ambition: to send his four sons and two daughters through college. He succeeded.

The father owned a private library of 7,000 volumes, and it was in the library that Willkie acquired the passion for reading which is still his chief hobby. His taste in books is almost universal, from poetry to economics, from philosophy to agriculture. And he brings to his reading a prodigious memory.

Some of the fruits of this memory were heard by America only lately, when Willkie proved to be one of the best informed guests ever to appear on the radio program *Information Please.*

His first law case came when he was sixteen, and it is notable that it was in defense of labor. He helped his father in a case in which the unions were fighting against an anti-picketing injunction.

On debating teams in school and college he was a passionate orator in defense of liberalism. He became a stanch follower of Robert M. La Follette.

He still considers himself so. Because his deepest conviction is the same as La Follette's: The heart of the American system is the control of power—the prevention of the accumulation of power in any hands at all.

Recently, on the debating platform with the younger La Follette, the latter lightly chided Willkie as an "economic royalist." Willkie came back:

"Here was your father's creed: 'To fight the system under which *Big Business* bought votes to install the tools of *Big Business* as judges, legislators, and administrators.' Mine is a parallel: 'To fight the system under which *Big Government* buys votes to install the tools of *Big Government* in office, so that its power over the country may be perpetuated.'"

Willkie had just opened his law offices when in 1917 America entered the World War. He enlisted on the day war was declared, and served as a first lieutenant with the 325th Field Artillery in France.

When he came back to America he joined with two partners in the firm of Mather, Nesbitt & Willkie, at Akron. The firm had several utilities companies among its clients. But while Willkie gave his share of time to their cases, he had other interests as well.

He led the battle in Akron against the Ku Klux Klan, which had seized much power there. And he went as a delegate to the Democratic Convention in 1924, so that he might oppose McAdoo. McAdoo had Klan support.

In 1929 Commonwealth & Southern induced Willkie to go to New York, and in 1933 he was elected president of the company. It was a dubious honor, because the utilities business was in terrible shape. The Insull scandals were in the air. Newspapers and politicians could attack the utilities as fearlessly as they might the man-eating shark or the boll weevil.

The sales of electrical current and the devices employing it—refrigerators and irons and so on—had hit rock bottom. Most companies were retrenching to the limit, cutting expenses to the bone.

Not so Willkie. He hired six hundred new salesmen. He offered plans to encourage the household use of electricity on liberal credit terms and began a big advertising campaign. In six years of that sort of salesmanship the amount of current sold by C. & S. for domestic use doubled and the rate was cut in half. The company today sells current for about one third less than the average for the country.

The company lost $1,600,000 in 1934. It made a profit of $10,600,000 in 1937. And that's what you call sound business management.

Got To Know America

It was while acting as a super-salesman that he got to know America, or that big slice of it served by his company. He went out on the road to cover his territory. About one third of each year he spent on the road, visiting every town of 2,000 or more in eleven states. He met everybody. And more than one Southern or Western newspaper said, with some astonishment, "Here is a genuine democrat, as approachable as a Pullman porter."

Willkie likes to talk; he also likes to listen. He does not believe in gag rules for either radicals or rock-ribbed conservatives. "There can never be too much agitation and criticism," he says. "If ideas are sound, they will bring improvement. If they are crackpot, they will die of their own weakness."

Such ideas as this made his colleagues in the utilities business a little nervous. They even challenged him with being hospitable to that bugaboo of the utilities, government ownership.

"No," he said; "I don't believe in it. I think it is wrong. But if the people want it they are going to have it, and they *should* have it."

His attacks upon the New Deal have struck where they hurt. He has charged dishonesty in thinking and performance, and backed up his assertions with fact. But his opposition to the administration does not spring from partisan bitterness nor from political ambitions of his own.

In 1932, having been a lifelong Democrat, he was one of the group supporting Newton D. Baker for the nomination which Roosevelt got. In 1936, for the first time, he voted a Republican ticket. But he does not approve of everything in the Republican Party, any more than he condemns everything in the New Deal.

Quite naturally, the New Deal has had its knives out for him. He has been openly threatened with revenge for his searing criticisms. And, to back up the threats, Washington has prowled into every nook and cranny of his business affairs and his private life—including, of course, income-tax returns, that mighty weapon which the government holds over citizens who show a tendency to step out of line.

They haven't found anything. Since becoming president of C. & S. Willkie has not bought or sold securities of his own or any other company. He has accepted no directorships in other corporations. His salary is $75,000 a year —low for the head of a billion-dollar concern —and he has consistently refused increases of pay or bonuses.

Liberalism, Democracy

But his concern for the future of America does not confine itself merely to attack upon the New Deal. Liberalism, democracy—these are his religion, and he has written down the creed of that religion in transparently clear terms.

There are no weasel words in his four main tenets:

1. The American system depends upon the limitation of power. It is just as bad for government to have unlimited power as for big business to be uncontrolled. (He has advocated government control of utilities since 1930.)

2. Business and industry are a vital part of the life of America. Government hatred and mistrust of them are fatal to the country's future. Private enterprise should be free to expand and enrich the existence of our citizens.

3. The government must, of course, spend on behalf of the people. But in spending there must be a businesslike approach: How to get the people the most for their money. Above all, the people must know exactly what their taxes are spent for.

4. In foreign affairs he is no isolationist. He opposes war and favors every common-sense measure to keep us out of it. But the United States cannot say, "We do not care what goes on in the rest of the world." Foreign trade is vital if we are to avoid government-regulated economy, government monopoly. He whole-heartedly favors the Hull trade agreements.

These are greatly condensed statements of his position. But of that position he says:

"This declaration will not interest those who regard the United States as a laboratory for social experiments.

"It will not interest those who regard the United States as a free-lunch counter.

"It will certainly not interest those who regard the United States as a somewhat impoverished gold mine out of which they can still scrape a nugget or two for themselves.

"It will interest only those who think of the United States as their land, a land that they know and love, a land that became rich through the industry, thrift, and enterprise of its people, and will never regain its prosperity in any other way."

His private life is simple. He is comfortably married, and has one son who will be graduated from Princeton this year. He doesn't play outdoor games or cards. He smokes cigarettes, and he takes a cocktail or highball whenever he feels like it. Vacation times, he goes to his Indiana farm.

Still Cracker Barrel

His contact with the great affairs of the world have polished him, of course. But the marks of the cracker barrel are still on him. He is big, and he loves men, and he is full of tremendous vitality. And talk is as necessary to him as water or food.

It must be good talk. Vain loud spouting is no part of his character. But it is perhaps his singular capacity to listen, plus the storehouse of ordered knowledge he possesses, plus the flexibility of his mind, which gives him such a vast advantage in the cockpit of political give and take.

It is the usual thing for good Americans to admire the forefathers. Willkie particularly cherishes Washington and Lincoln and Robert E. Lee—for one particular remark that each of them made:

Washington: "Without more charity for the opinions and acts of one another in governmental matters, I believe it will be difficult, if not impracticable, to manage the reins of government, or to keep the parts of it together."

Lee: "I have fought against the people of the North because I believe they were trying to wrest from the South dearest rights. But I have never cherished toward them bitter or vindictive feelings, and have never seen the day when I did not pray for them."

Lincoln: "With malice toward none; with charity for all."

He resolves these three philosophies into one of his own: "Just as the true liberals of the world have a common purpose, so they have a common quality. That quality is love of humankind. The true liberal does not fight for a cause from a desire to punish those who have a different way of looking at things and doing things. Instead, the true liberal fights for a cause which he feels will be of much value to his opponents as to himself."

It is his most searing charge against the New Deal that hatred and, indeed, malice toward some, have guided most of its actions.

These are the things he loves to talk about, his feet on the desk, hard by Wall Street. You can smell the old cracker barrel and feel the warmth of the old iron-bellied stove as the words come eloquently off his tongue. And perhaps that is the reason Wall Street is wary of him and wishes that he would shut up and have done. Wall Street doesn't like American liberalism and democracy spouted from the cracker barrel.

The Willkie boom may evaporate as automatically as it started. Certainly it will not be kept alive by any of the usual political routine —by any activity at all from the man at the center of it. But, President or not, a great many Americans are going to be heartened by the presence of a man like Willkie in the land.

Willkie had a talent for photogenic poses.

A Third Term for Fear

by Clare Boothe

Clare Boothe was a Republican congress-woman from Connecticut, later ambassador to Italy, wife of publisher Henry Luce, and playwright. She told why she supported Willkie in 1940.

I was in France when the war was called "phony." I was in Holland and Belgium when the blitzkrieg came, and I saw the heartbreaking collapse of France, and England, unbelievably surprised, waiting in sudden horror and shock for its own ordeal by bomb and fire. I saw Europe go up in flames and the men, women, and children, and all their old ways of life pass into that condtion of hell called Total War.

Because I have seen these things, I feel more strongly than I have ever before felt anything about my own country that Wendell Willkie should be elected its President.

I believe that he should be elected President because he expresses the faith of a small, sadly dwindling band of men and women—the rash, bold, courageous, unpopular faith that *democrarcy has not yet failed*. This band of men and women believes rather that Europe failed democracy and that we are in grave danger of doing the same.

In Europe in the spring you heard Frenchmen, Dutchmen, Norwegians, Belgians, of *all* classes, say more often than they said anything else, "Of course, you realize, no matter how this war turns out, democracy has failed." How *could* it turn out other than it did, if they believed that?

This fear that democracy was doomed was what counseled France's leaders to sell out fast and easy to Fascism.

When I returned to my country in late June, I had looked forward with pride and certainty to finding a great country whose true democratic spirit, awakened by the tragedy of Europe's lost democracy, would be fighting to breathe vigorous life and confidence into its own democracy.

But I found instead a nation that was almost hysterically afraid. The witless ones, of course, feared a German invasion in the morning. Many people feared that no matter when the invasion came, we would not be "armed in time."

Need Spiritual Arming

Now, come Willkie, or Roosevelt again, we will be *materially* armed in time. But our material arms will do us no good if, like the French, we are spiritually unarmed, spiritually stricken already to our knees by the fear that "democracy anyhow is bound to fail."

And I saw at once that in America, as in France, this was the fundamental doubt, the deep fear in many American hearts. And that, whether we admitted it or not, this was the issue we would all vote on when we went in November to the polls.

Back in 1933, in his inaugural address, Franklin Roosevelt said one thing I shall never forget —no one should ever forget. He said, "There is nothing to fear but fear."

Now years have passed. And I say—though Mr. Roosevelt no longer does—there is *still* nothing for Americans to fear but *fear*. Mr. Roosevelt no longer says it, perhaps because Mr. Roosevelt has nothing to hope for for *himself* but our fears. Here is the charge I make: Mr. Roosevelt is seeking re-election on a platform of ignoble fears. Almost without exception, those who will vote for him are *the people who are afraid*—

People who are afraid that they may be taken off relief. People who are afraid that they will have to go on relief soon (i. e., that the "system" has permanently broken down). People who are afraid (being ignorant of the true and proper powers of a President) that the army and navy will suddenly fall apart if Mr. Roosevelt is not there. People who are afraid for racial reasons—strangely, tragically doubting the true spirit of America which is the property of *no* party—the spirit of tolerance.

People who are afraid that Hitler will be less afraid of Willkie than of Roosevelt. People who are afraid to "swap horses in mid-stream." (This was the fear that kept Daladier in power until it was too late—that kept Chamberlain in power until all was nearly lost.) Intellectuals who are afraid that with "democracy absolutely finished," Willkie is the road to a "bloody revolution," whereas Roosevelt is the perhaps painless bridge to their "inevitable Socialism." People—and this represents the majority, perhaps, of the Third Termers—who are just plain scared out of their seven senses of *anything* unfamiliar or unknown which the future may hold. People who are afraid to elect any man President who has not had "great experience in that office before." And all the people—*all* the people—who no longer trust themselves or their country or the traditions and beliefs which have made that country great through thirty-three Presidencies.

Wendell Willkie has chosen to put his emphasis on courage and confidence. Politicians are not generally noted for their courage. But here was Mr. Willkie, a man seeking the Presidency against a formidable foe, who was not afraid to chuck overboard the sizable Isolationist vote of this country because he believed America could not longer be isolated from the affairs of the troubled world; a man who was not afraid to give comfort and ammunition to his enemy by saying he believed in many of the New Deal social objectives; a man who refused to delay conscription, although many politicians told him by doing so he would make a useful political issue of it; a man who subscribed to more and more aid to Britain, although he knew that for that aid his rival would get most of the credit. A man, in short, who was not afraid to debate, talk like a rational man, giving credit, even to the opposition, where credit was due.

Against such a rational, honest procedure he was counseled by the "politicians." But courage scorns all the counsels which are inspired by fear. But the thing Mr. Willkie has the courage to say which Mr. Roosevelt has not got the courage—or perhaps the conviction—to say was that he still believes in the material and spiritual progress of this country along old-fashioned, American, democratic lines.

The keystone of Willkie's policy is courage and faith. Faith that America is still a free land, with possibilities of expansion, wealth, strength, and happiness heretofore undreamed of—if we only have the courage to try once again. Willkie has faith that it is well within our power to set our house in order and to defend it. And that we need not sell it out today or tomorrow to a Fascist or Communist or Socialist landlord, even though he would come wearing a false beard, looking ever so much, at first, like our tough and generous and beloved and free Uncle Sam.

Noted writer and politician Clare Boothe, a staunch Willkie supporter.

This Urgent Now

by Fannie Hurst

Writer Fannie Hurst favored continuing the Roosevelt administration in 1940. These were her reasons for favoring a third term.

Fannie Hurst with Sen. Robert Wagner.

Tradition is an elegant and impressive noun. At present, however, it is sticking out like a sore thumb from the colloquial vocabulary of the average American.

In its pedestrian stride, tradition is something that comes down, usually by word of mouth, from one generation to another. By happy survival of the fittest, most tradition is a residuum of the best in human thinking and behavior that has percolated through time.

But tradition is not inviolate. There is such a thing as the obsolescence of tradition. The dead past should very often remain that way. Arbitrary the tradition that will not admit the exception to its rule.

Now, this no-third term tradition of ours (long may it wave, as a general rule) has run into its exception. That exception is this urgent Now.

I am for a continuation of the present adminstration because I believe (its various shortcomings to the contrary notwithstanding) that this country at this time has everything to gain by continuation under a leader whose domestic and international policies have held us together during a period of years when world disintegration rages about us.

I say this in full awareness of the hardships that have been automatically imposed upon certain economic classes in American life. I say this, full of awareness of arbitrary conditions in our government which have been the dual result of the personality of our President, but, more than that, the result of the personality of our kind of emergency—an emergency which has been endemic during these eight years.

Realizing all this, I still believe that the big and little business man in America today is looking down his nose, an optical contortion which is deadly to clear vision. His pocket nerve is hurting. With some justification, he sees not only his functioning world adumbrated, but, because of his personal discomfort, would throw the entire administration's achievements into the discard.

It is difficult for this business man to evaluate the colossal fact that for eight years this administration has been steering us through a social revolution, bloodlessly, without bastille, pillage, or faces in red mud. Contemplating some of these more usual accessories of social revolution, the twitching pocket nerve should seem relatively trivial.

I am not only for this liberalizing and liberating administration because of what I believe will be its enduring and historic contribution in such vital fields as collective bargaining, social security, soil conservation, housing, and many other New Deal social innovations, I am for the New Deal because I think longer vision will show it up to be an all-around Big Deal, even for those who feel most put upon.

This brings up sharply consideration of the alleged dictatorship of President Roosevelt. Certainly he has been called upon, during his tempestuous administration of unprecedented events, to abrogate, meet emergencies, and do his own creative thinking. But remember, there is always a check on Presidential powers. The President can only do what Congress gives him the right to do, and the power of legislation-giving is matched by the Congressional ability to take away.

Congress can enact any law it pleases, and whenever a two-thirds majority in Congress chooses, it can nullify any Presidential veto.

In all the destructive and deplorable ragings of political animosities which are consuming our country while Rome burns, I have yet to hear anything approaching a sustained and corrective program offered by the anti-administration factions.

Glittering generalities glitter. We are promised a better world of paid-up bills, economic adjustment, prosperity, jobs, production, but no one bothers to be definitive.

"We have scarcely begun to know," states the opposition, "what we can do with our resources and our man power." So what? Obviously we have the resources and the man power, but the method of harnessing them is what the average American today, whom we shall call John Smith, needs to know, and what the nation needs to know before entrusting itself to the campaign rhetoric of a new and untried candidate. We do not need a mining engineer to tell us that we have gold in them thar hills. We do need one to get it out!

This is not to say that the present administration has succeeded in mining it. But certainly the majority of the Mr. and Mrs. John Smiths of this country have in the past eight years been the recipients of concentrated effort on the part of their government to make their world a better place in which to live, to improve their homes, fill their dinner pails, educate their children, and provide more of the good things of life which hitherto have not been allowed to fall their way. If Mr. and Mrs. Smith are as astute as they need to be, they will have confidence in the continued constructive behaviorism of such an administration.

This is the end of an era, Mr. and Mrs. Smith, and don't you forget it. Forces stronger than economics are at work. The social readjustments that the world needs to make have not to do primarily even with the administration, any more than the Weather Bureau creates the weather it reports.

This administration is on to this fact, just as it is on to the fact that the era is changing hands. Forces bigger than the biggest New Deal conceivable are forcing the hand of big business, little business, capital, and labor. Those eight years the administration has been steering in a gale, in mid-channel, surrounded on all sides by a rocky social and industrial archipelago.

This urgent Now, which justifies the third-term emergency, is not the time to change boats!

The dog in Aesop's fable dropped his piece of meat for what he saw reflected in the water.

By now his ribs must be poking through.

Fannie Hurst (second from right), a Roosevelt supporter, with Eleanor Roosevelt (seated) and Mrs. William Randolph Hearst (left).

Why Hitler Watched Our Election

by Wythe Williams

How Hitler attempted to influence the 1940 elections is described in this November 1940 article from Liberty Magazine.

We can smash any combination of French and British armies. We need not fear British sea power. We must, however, drive a permanent wedge between London and Washington. The United States of America alone defeated us in 1918."

Speaker: Adolf Hitler.

Place: A room in the Bürger braukeller, Munich.

Time: 1923.

What Hitler the demagogue said seventeen years ago still holds good with the Hitler of today. It has remained his firm conviction that what caused the defeat of Imperial Germany in 1918 was the financial and industrial power of the United States.

All along, he has kept a watchful eye on the American political situation. The Reich Foreign Ministry in Berlin maintains an American Information Section with a permanent staff of 850 experts who sift a never-ending stream of information gathered by German diplomatic and political observers in the United States. This information is boiled down into concise weekly reports. These are submitted to Foreign Minister von Ribbentrop and, with his comments, are passed on to Hitler. It is on the basis of these reports that Hitler makes his decisions, insofar as they may affect the attitude of the United States.

Who Is "This Man Willkie"?

The American political event of last June burst upon them with the force of a bombshell. In opposition to President Roosevelt they had expected the nomination of a run-of-the-mill politician. Within twenty-four hours after the nomination of Mr. Willkie, a 20,000-word report was radioed to Berlin from the German Embassy at Washington, detailing the life story of the candidate from early childhood. Hitler's program in Europe had been largely based on the assumption that public opinion in the United States during election year would be too divided for the rendering of any effective military assistance to England and France. Now Hitler himself demanded to know about "this man Willkie."

It took the Reich Foreign Ministry almost three weeks to bring the stream of data on the new situation into comprehensive shape. The result found its way to Ribbentrop's desk in the form of a 200-page dossier. He devoted several days to personal study of it before passing it on to Propaganda Minister Goebbels, with eighteen typewritten pages of his observations and recommendations attached to it. The entire report was then turned over to the American section of Goebbels' propaganda institution. Early in August it appeared on Goebbels' desk.

Now for excerpts from the comments by Ribbentrop and Goebbels, as attached to this dossier when it was placed on Hitler's desk on August 10. How these quotations, also the quotation of Hitler's own words which I give later, became available to me cannot be told before the war is over. To do so would immediately endanger a man's life. Here are the comments by Ribbentrop:

"Our policy with respect to the United States must be dictated by our economic and racial interests in the various republics of South America. These interests form part of the greater living space of the Germanic race. . . . As during the World War, so today the United States is engaged in an effort to rob the German people of the fruits of many years of hard pioneer work and farsighted planning by their

compatriots in South America. . . .

"The political situation in the United States is almost analogous to that which prevailed in France a year ago and for a number of years before that. We have drawn every possible advantage from the French situation. Considering the American population factor, we should do even better in the case of the United States. . . .

"More seeds for internal disunity have been planted in the United States than at any time since the Civil War. . . . The nation is in the throes of a class struggle. If nourished, it will engender more bitterness than any struggle of nationalities. . . . The National Socialist Reich is presented here with a unique opportunity. . . .

"All information of the past month bears out the original report that the surprising nomination of this man Willkie came in response to a sort of popular demand. He calls himself 'the people's choice,' and to a certain extent he may be correct. Such a situation is fraught with potential danger. No brake must be put upon the class struggle, at least until the people are confronted with new disillusionment. . . . The interests of the National Socialist Reich will be served admirably by an intensification of the class struggle in the United States."

Now for typical excerpts from Goebbels' written recommendations:

"The promotion of national disunity in the United States should dominate all other considerations. We should not be content with accentuating the present class struggle in America. Considering the heterogeneous composition of the people who call themselves Americans, every effort must be undertaken to pit the various component nationalities against one another. . . .

"Tactics of the past years have left deep scars on the American mind. These scars should be reopened. An emotional free-for-all among the American people is in the interest of the National Socialist Reich. . . . Apart from the traditional American cleavages, we find today a veritable hodge-podge of divisions. Powerful interests are clamoring for war as opposed to the convinced pacifists—vigorous activists in the field of foreign policy as against confirmed isolationists—protagonists of centralized power by the State as against advocates of individual

liberty. . . . Never before in the history of the United States have so many pressure groups opposed one another. . . .

"This man Willkie comes from native German stock in the third generation. He should have the sacred interests of the German people at heart. But he may turn out one of the leading antagonists of the National Socialist Reich. Then there would be nothing to choose between him and Franklin Roosevelt.

"In close co-operation with our Italian and Russian allies on this issue, we should give guidance to an absolute minimum of six million American votes. The great majority of these are in the key states of New York, Pennsylvania, Ohio, Michigan, Illinois, and Wisconsin. In these circumstances it should not be difficult to influence the result of the election so as to serve the overseas interests of the National Socialist Reich."

Nazi Agents Instructed

Hitler, after receiving the voluminous document on August 10, took it to Berchtesgaden. He waited until August 19 to render his verdict, after reading the Willkie acceptance speech at Elwood. It came in the form of personal instructions attached to the dossier. These, together with the excerpts by Ribbentrop and Goebbels, were instantly forwarded to Washington, whence they were distributed among Nazi agents throughout the United States.

"My instructions must be carried out in spirit as well as in letter. . . . But every semblance of interference by the National Socialist Reich in the American election campaign must be meticulously avoided. In the event of a misstep, the Reich government will disclaim all knowledge of the matter. The work must be carried out by local groups interested exclusively in the future welfare of the United States. [! ! !] The Reich government will help indirectly and constantly, and before Election Day the name of the candidate for whom every vote must be cast will be communicated."

Adolf Hitler's amazing accomplishments as a political quick-change artist are now known to all the world. This time, however, as shown by the ending of his instructions, which proves his own uncertainty, it is entirely possible that he has out-in-trigued even himself.

Democracy Reaps the Whirlwind

by Mayling Soong Chiang

The author of the following article published in December 1940 is the American-educated wife of Chinese Generalissimo Chiang Kai-shek.

There is nothing like a great conflagration to clear the way for large-scale city improvement, and there is perhaps nothing like a war such as we in China have been waging in self-defense to prepare the way for a far-reaching remolding of our national character in particular and and our national life in general.

The fires of war have burned into our soul— and blazoned upon the sky for all who have eyes to see—some startling revelations and unexpected changes. Political disunity disappeared in a flash before Japanese aggression. More important, the physical and moral cowardice which was supposed to be born and bred in our bones and blood faded as if by magic. Instead of ancient China falling prostrate and groveling before the Japanese invaders, China's ill-armed people, unsupported by other nations, stood on their feet in stalwart defiance, and were mowed down in their millions by the most ferocious and inhumane type of warfare that had ever been let loose upon human beings.

The Japanese invented and applied the "total" warfare now known as "blitzkrieg." But, for three long years and more, the Chinese people have shown the world how to face and endure it. Truly a miracle, if ever a miracle has, in contemporary times, been chronicled. And if one miracle is possible, why not another?

This thought has led me to make an attempt to stimulate my compartiots to reform by laying bare certain evils within our country which became inherent solely because they were of benefit to the old-time official class, and have been tolerated up to this period because no one

Mayling Soong Chiang, Mme. Chiang Kai-shek.

cared publicly to condemn them. What I should not like to see is that foreign readers of translations of my writings should gain the impression that I hold our people solely responsible for all that is wrong with China, or imply that what is right with China is due solely to foreign influence. Far from it.

Abandoned By Friends

Occidental science, technique, and learning of all kinds have conferred great benefits upon China. We have still much more to draw from the founts of foreign knowledge. But my countrymen probably would not agree, after these three tragic years of unrestrained desolation of their land, that much that is good or wise could be learned from the equivocal evolution, as they have witnessed it, of foreign policy. In fact, some rather strong views upon that subject are being entertained, and, since I have been free in pillorying the pet peccadilloes of our people for foreign edification, they consider it incumbent upon me to express their feelings and reactions with regard, at least, to the value of foreign promises and performances in the field of international politics.

Democratic statesmen have fallen far short of that lofty ideal of honorable recognition and fulfillment of obligations that has been set up before our people. Treaties, agreements, and understandings have gone with the wind of self-interest, and, so far as we of China are concerned, we have been virtually abandoned, and even victimized, by those in high authority whom we had been taught we could regard with unshaken confidence as our friends. To our people it is unutterably sad that for three weary, heartbreaking years of heroic resistance we have been left without help to combat a savage aggressor in a war which is not ours alone but which is that of all democracies.

It is painful to have to say that my countrymen, rightly or wrongly, have been forced by their terrible experiences to a conclusion derogatory to respect for the democracies. The people of China are convinced that the warfare now cleaving Europe and shocking the whole world is directly due to failure of the democracies to appraise correctly the character and intentions of Japan.

Violation of Treaties

It is the opinion of the Chinese people, too, that the negative attitude of the democracies toward Japanese aggression in China constituted a violation of treaties and international undertakings which was as reprehensible and as disastrous to international honor and good faith as the positive abrogations and acts of violence of which Japan was guilty when she invaded Manchuria in September, 1931, and China proper in July, 1937.

Japan's easy conquest of Manchuria by unscrupulous means was but an example of how an aggressor could safely kick irksome principles into limbo and survive unscathed to enjoy only the possession of the "conquered" territory, but also the continued political, economic, and social good will and friendship of those democratic nations which were originally the most vociferous in their denunciation of the aggression. Japan had tested international

reactions to undeclared warfare, to the wholesale abrogation of treaties; and she found them empty of danger—either immediate or remote.

What other encouragement did the militarists of Japan require to set about tackling China? None. When her plans were perfected for further outrage she expanded the "Manchurian Incident" into the "North China Incident," and that, in turn, into the "China Incident." Soon it promises to assume the stature of an "Asia Incident."

When Japan invaded Manchuria we refrained from resisting because the League of Nations undertook to adjust matters. They lost the region for us. There was a difference, however, when the Japanese proceeded to invade China proper. Then we abandoned faith in international undertakings, and we fought. For more than three years now Japan has been gouging with ferocious intensity at the very vitals of our country. She set the example for the wholesale slaughter and destruction now running riot in Europe—an example that might never have materialized had the democracies only fulfilled their obligations to China by restraining Japan. Penalization of Japan would have nipped aggression in the bud. The pity of it is that up to now there has been no actual punishment, nor has there been any rebuke for her impertinencies, her trespasses upon the rights of the democracies, or her bellicose bluffing.

No One Ready To Fight

Without any appreciable aid from the democracies, which professed to be horrified, the people of China have suffered hardships such as no other race on earth has ever been called upon to endure. We have survived the ordeal; and, contrary to all preconceived ideas entertained by foreigners claiming expert knowledge of China, we have succeeded in inflicting punishment in full measure upon the Japanese, and in bogging down their colossal military machine in our vast hinterland.

For those three years, however, the Chinese people saw the professed defenders of international law and order failing to come to our aid or even to support our cause openly. We know the explanation, the excuse—that no one was ready to fight. Nor were we; but we fought. Think what would have been the situation in the world today had we refrained from defending ourselves, had we surrendered.

Those nations who were expected to employ every means in their power to defend right against might have made it abundantly clear to the Chinese people that they would not openly help to defend anything—in Asia. On the contrary, they seemed to be striving to avoid difficulties by obeying the dictates of Japan. The American government ordered airplanes, bought by China before the opening of hostilities, to be removed from an American steamer then at a port on the west coast of the United States; the Australian government refused to permit even the parts of a private passenger airplane to be assembled in Sydney and flown to China. But both countries eagerly supplied war materials to Japan. The British and French governments were meticulous in avoiding actions calculated to give umbrage to Japan. The British government refused to allow British military or air experts to aid China; the American government threatened its technical instructors working with the Chinese Air Force with loss of citizenship. A similar fate was to befall any American who volunteered to fight in the air for China. Yet quite a contrary policy was pursued with regard to the war in Spain.

All this our people had before their eyes while they saw their homes being blown to pieces and their fellow beings slaughtered, robbed, impoverished, or made victims of opium.

The continued willingness of the democracies to regard Japan as an equal, to shake the bloodstained hands of her ambassadors, to court her trade emissaries, while lodging futile and empty face-saving protests which did not save any one's face, presented an astonishing spectacle to the Chinese people, and encouraged the Japanese to laugh up their sleeves while they flouted the protests. It was no wonder to our people that Japan refused any longer to respect or fear the democracies.

France capitulated to Japan's pressure, and the route of supplies through Indo-China was closed with the suddenness of a pinpricked balloon; Great Britain vainly attempted to appease Japan by the temporary closing of the Burma Road. And America? It was three years before America did so much (although now she has recently done somewhat more) as to place

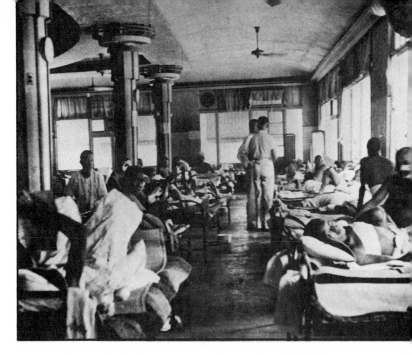

Above: Wounded Chinese soldiers crowd a Shanghai cabaret turned hospital. Below: Japanese soldiers shooting at Chinese in Shanghai.

a controlling hand upon the sale to Japan of scrap steel and aviation gasoline; and even that was done with the cautious explanation that this measure was adopted merely for the sake of self-defense, and was not necessarily aimed specially at Japan.

This has led the Chinese people to think that America could not in any wise explain away her attitude of the past three years, for it must be remembered that while impartial, justice-loving Americans did try to do all they could to point out the significance of China's struggle and aid China in relief work, others in America amassed profits by selling to Japan the necessities of warfare. Eighty per cent of Japan's war supplies came from America—and 95 per cent of the aviation gasoline which was used by Japan in her ruthless bombing was American.

China Crippled Japan

China has thus been compelled to fight a war not of her own making with a Power which has been aided and abetted unstintingly by the markets of the democracies. These markets were virtually closed to us, for no help was given us to avail ourselves of them. China has been the champion of the principles for which other democracies are now at war, but mention of what China has been able to do for the cause is seldom if ever made—an amazing situation.

If China has done nothing else, she has at least crippled the might of Japan so that Japan cannot swiftly fulfill the program long ago revealed in the notorious Tanaka Memorial for securing the hegemony of Asia and the domination of the whole Pacific. With her army, her air force, and with her navy intact, and with no such millstone round her neck as a tenacious and resisting China, Japan would have been able with consumate ease to destroy British, French, and American power in Asia.

Our people feel that America, instead of giving any further assistance to Japan, should fully recognize the debt she owes to them for keeping occupied in China 3,000,000 men of the Japanese army, including those killed and wounded, thus giving America time to catch her breath and strengthen her defenses. That it has been recognized by the democracies so tardily and honored so incompletely is causing our people to feel more and more that, if China's rights and contributions continue to be ignored, China will be forced in the future so to conduct herself that the democratic governments may know that if she could get along without them in the turmoil of war, she can get along without them in the less perilous times of peace.

This would be a regrettable attitude for China to be constrained to adopt, since it has always been felt by intelligent Chinese that the destiny of their country lies with the democracies. I have personally expressed that conviction time and again.

It should be pointed out, however, that the trend of thought of our people toward a revision of their ideas of the value of association with the democracies is not the product of momentary fancy, nor has it been molded in any way by the startling and unexpected events in Europe. Whatever change of thought may take place will be born of the realization of democratic inadequacy in defending proclaimed principles; plus the studied refusal to treat Japan as an aggressor; plus the apparently considered refusal to credit China with her unprecedented contribution to democratic stability and defense; plus the absence of free and fair acknowledgement of her help, of her great and grievous sacrifices in fighting aggression and thus upholding democratic principles.

This list of delinquencies of the democracies cannot in any way be ascribed to that spurious wisdom which often comes after the maturity of an event. Space does not allow me to quote the many warnings I have uttered during the past three years with regard to the serious consequences of the indifference of the democracies to happenings in China. That these Cassandran prophecies have come true is no more gratifying to us in China than it must be to the democracies who have sown the wind and are now reaping the remorseless whirlwind.

Intellectual honesty constrains me to point out that throughout the first three years of resistance Soviet Russia extended to China, for the actual purchase of war materials and other necessities, credits several times larger in amount than the credits given by either Great Britain or America. Both these countries, indeed, circumscribed their advances with conditions which prevented even one cent of the money being used for badly needed munitions, equipment, or war material of any kind. Furthermore, at the meetings of the League of Nations, it was Russia who took an uncompromising stand in support of China's appeal that active measures should be adopted to brand Japan as the aggressor. Russia acted similarly during the Brussels Conference. On both occasions Britain, France, and other member nations compromised their consciences. When Japan protested through her ambassador in Moscow that the aid extended to China by Russia was a breach of neutrality, Russia did not wilt, or surrender, or compromise, but continued to send supplies of arms to China.

It will doubtless be said that Russia has been aiding China for selfish interests. In reply to this I may point out that Russian help has been unconditional; that China has never asked any nation to fight for her. And, I may add, if democracy is to survive the policy of "One for one and all for none," statesmanlike foresight should see that it is replaced with the policy of "One for all and all for one."

A Bitter Lesson

What has happened, however—and what has not happened—is another great lesson to the Chinese people, another bitter lesson that they will never forget. They will remember never to believe in international promises, no matter how many imposing seals adorn the documents.

One thing they have been taught is that China must aim, in her future national development, at attaining self-reliance. She will have to devise means so that for all time she will not need to depend upon others. I have been trying to emphasize this idea in the training of my students, so that they might have competency and be capable of facing life without fear. If the war should end tomorrow, a firm foundation on this score can be erected by any one who is not afraid of hard work.

What the future holds no one can tell, of course. If, unhappily for the democracies as well as for China, we should be defeated in the end, at least the world ought to know that we were beaten not because of lack of courage—either moral or physical—but because China was strangled to death by an economic noose fashioned by Japan out of British appeasement, American profiteering, and French fear.

The spirit of China is unconquerable. Whatever happens, we will prove our valor and our honor. An old-fashioned word—honor, yet a word of sterling worth. It has suffered an eclipse, or a partial eclipse, in international relationship for some years, but we hope to see it emerge again shining like a lustrous beacon.

To all the citizens of the democracies who have given their time, their substance, and their sympathy to succor and encourage the millions of stricken ones in our country, goes out the abiding gratitude of the Chinese people.

Japanese troops prepare to sail to Manchuria.

Our Friendship With America

by Winston Churchill

Winston Churchill's magnificent prose was turned in May 1941 to the subject of Anglo-American Friendship, "the majestic edifice."

It is a relief to turn from the quarrels and jealousies of distracted Europe to contemplate the majestic edifice of Anglo-American friendship.

We can best serve the cause of Anglo-American friendship if we examine the past as well as the present.

The founders of America fled from Britain to escape persecution. Tyranny—or what can be more disastrous than tyranny, a purblind, pettifogging legalism—pursued them across the Atlantic.

Taxed by men they had never seen, sitting in a Parliament in whose deliberations they had no voice, the descendants of the Pilgrim Fathers and the Virginian Cavaliers raised, together, the standard of revolt.

But we forget—and America remembers—that the first shots in the War of Independence were fired by British troops—"unmolested and unprovoked," says the contemporary Massachusetts Spy—on men who offered no resistance.

The long war, in which German mercenaries were lavishly if unsuccessfully employed, was ended by a grudging peace. Suspicion and bitterness remained.

France beheaded a king—and crowned an emperor whose armies trampled the map of Europe. At death grips with Napoleon, Britain blockaded the coast of the United States, seized American ships, and pressed American sailors into service on her men-o'-war.

The resulting War of 1812 to 1815 was to Britain only a vexatious diversion. But it was a life-and-death struggle to the United States, and its incidents left an indelible impression on the American mind.

Indian tribes, fighting as allies of England, killed and ravaged. Fort Dearborn, on the site where Chicago now stands, was stormed by painted savages and the entire garrison massacred. Women and children were murdered.

A British fleet sailed up the Potomac to Washington, burned the Capitol and the government offices and the President's house.

It is doubtful if one in ten thousand of our population has ever heard of that raid of reprisals.

But we should remember—vividly—for centuries after the event, if London were, even for a day, in the hands of an American force that destroyed Buckingham Palace, the Houses of Parliament, Whitehall, and Downing Street.

True, we should also remember the strong ties of blood and race that bound the Americans and ourselves. But might not these make the injury all the worse?

Roosevelt and Churchill at Casablanca, 1943.

We have done terrible things to each other through misunderstanding. Odious chapters of our common history are stained with blood and the hatreds that are fed by blood. Wrongs, revenges, insults, calumnies, battles, and executions crowd the pages, with noble, suffering, or conquering figures silhouetted against the dull red haze.

To us, however, these conflicts have, as a rule, been side issues. That has helped us to forget. And sometimes we have wanted to forget because we were ashamed.

But America was concerned more vitally, and some of the most glorious episodes of her history are bound up with these tragic happenings. So Americans have a double reason to remember. The cheers of vanished armies, the rumbling of long-silenced cannonades still come down to them today.

We must remember that for over a century America has attracted immigrants not only from Britain but from all Europe. There is a great German population in the Middle West. Swedes and Italians are to be found everywhere. Of every hundred American citizens, nine are Negroes. Practically every nation on earth has contributed its quota to this vast melting pot.

These foreign elements may learn to speak English, but will they think English thoughts?

Though those of European stock may be fused into the nation of their adoption and become "hundred-percent Americans," it can only be by processes which tend to separate the American mind from ours.

Yet when all has been urged and weighed it still remains true that the conceptions which unite us are incomparably stronger than those that divide; that they are vital, not morbid; that they embrace the future rather than the past.

The mischances of history have riven and sundered us, but our roots lie deep in the same rich soil. The great Republic of the West, no less than the British Empire, sprang from the loins of Shakespeare's England. The beginnings of American history are to be found not across the Atlantic but where the Thames flows between green lawns and woodlands down to a gray sea.

Britain and America are joint sharers in a great inheritance of law and letters. Our political institutions, under the mask of outward difference, bear the marks of a common origin and a common aim.

Tie Of Language

We are both democracies—and today our countries are the last great strongholds of parliamentary government and individual liberty.

It is the English-speaking nations who, almost alone, keep alight the torch of Freedom.

These things are a powerful incentive to collaboration. With nations, as with individuals, if you care deeply for the same things, and these things are threatened, it is natural to work together to preserve them.

Words cannot be effaced by time. The greatest tie of all is *language*. There is nothing like that.

Ancient alliances, solemn treaties, faithful services given and repaid, important mutual interests—not all these taken together are equal, or nearly equal, to the bond of a common tongue.

Words are the only things that last forever. The most tremendous monuments or prodigies of engineering crumble under the hand of time. The Pyramids molder, the bridges rust, the canals fill up, grass covers the railway track; but words spoken two or three thousand years ago remain with us now, not as mere relics of the past but with all their pristine vital force.

Leaping across the gulf of time, they light the world for us today.

It is this power of words—words written in the past; words spoken at this moment; words printed in the newspapers; words sent speeding through the ether in a transatlantic broadcast; the flashing interchange of thought—that is our principal agency of union. Its work must continue indefinitely—will continue, indeed, on an ever larger scale.

With every new school that is opened, with every book that is printed, with every improvement in travel, with every film, with every record, identity of language gathers greater power and applies its processes more often to more people.

It is for us to see that this great lever of a common language is rightly used. We must employ it to explore and, so far as possible, compose the differences between us, and to bring to the surface our underlying identity of outlook and purpose.

Above all, we must use it to understand each other.

Teach American History

We, on this side of the Atlantic, know too little of American history. Not only are we ignorant of the full extent of our past quarrels with the United States, but we have only the most superficial comprehension of that great westward drive which carried civilization across a continent.

We have heard of Buffalo Bill. Thanks to The Plainsman, we have been introduced to Wild Bill Hickok. But we see the story through a reducing glass.

The Odyssey of a people has been an individual adventure; the epic has been dwarfed to the proportions of a fairy tale.

We talk glibly of the Monroe Doctrine. How many of us understand it? How many of us realize that for over a hundred years the United States has been the guarantor of the whole of the Western Hemisphere against aggression from without?

Such is the practical effect of the Monroe Doctrine.

I should like to see American history taught in our school concurrently with our own island story. It might help to correct the popular idea of the United States as a land of money-grubbers and multiple divorces.

But that conception should also be assailed directly. No doubt there is a certain excuse for it. It is easier to secure a divorce in certain American states than it is here.

The American divorce law is merely the logical development of ideas held nearly 400 years ago by the first Protestant Archbishop of Canterbury, and in the seventeenth century by the English Puritans.

Divorce, however, may be available for those who desire it without affecting the permanence of marriage.

For the vast majority of Americans, as for the vast majority of British people, marriage is a contract for life, a partnership which only death dissolves.

The charge of money-grubbing arises directly from the needs and circumstances of a dynam-·

John Paul Jones captures British warship.

57

ically expanding society. The great tasks which Americans have set themselves for a century have been in the economic field.

Utilize A Continent

Washington, Hamilton, Jefferson, Jackson, Adams, and Marshall—these men, soldiers, statesmen, lawyers, made a nation. They fashioned the instruments of government and established lines on which American politics were to develop.

But when they leave the stage the searchlight of history wheels—save for the years of the Civil War—to the struggle to subdue and utilize a continent.

That struggle has necessarily and rightly taken the first place in the life of the Amercan people. So business to the American is more than the means of earning a living or making a fortune; it is that career of interest, ambition, possibly even glory, which in the older world is afforded by the learned professions and state services, military and civilian.

A young American wishing to play a worthy part in the control of affairs directs himself instinctively toward the managing of factories, railroads, banks, stores, or some other of the thousand and one varieties of industrial or commercial enterprise.

Practically all the prizes of American life are to be gained in business. There, too, is the main path of useful service to the nation. Nearly all that is best and most active in the manhood and ability of the United States goes into business with the same sense of serving the country as a son of an old family in England might enter Parliament.

It is this concentration of American talent on business that has gained for the United States the title, The Land of the Dollar.

But, for the best type of Americans, dollars have been a by-product in business activity rather than its main aim.

On the other hand, dollars have played too great a part in American politics.

It is as a result of this that today, when the phase of intensive economic expansion is over, the flower of American manhood still regards the political scene with suspicion and distaste.

We, in this country, must try to understand these things, just as we must seek to correct American misconceptions of England.

Some of these are already being corrected. Americans have learned by bitter experience that to provide for the casualties of civilization by means of social insurance is not necessarily the sign of an effete society.

Personal Contact Important

There are many ways in which both countries might, with advantage, learn from each other.

It is encouraging that so many American books are being read in England and so many English books in America. The literature of a nation is the best interpreter of its spirit. Reading each other's books, we come to appreciate more clearly our fundamental kinship, and to see our differences in truer perspective.

The best British and American films carry this work of mutual illumination a stage farther.

But direct personal contact is still of the first importance. We cannot dispense with it.

British lecture tours in America have been of immense value in this respect. They have taken a number of people from this side of the Atlantic—myself among them—over a considerable part of the American continent and enabled them to meet large numbers of American citizens of varying types.

These Americans have thus learned something of England; the lecturers have brought home with them a new and truer picture of America.

The friendliness of Americans to the traveler from Britain, their unfailing kindliness, their generous hospitality, are something to marvel at.

In spite of "British reserve," some of us manage to make friends. Ties are formed strong enough to defy time and distance. We cherish pleasant memories of American homes, and they of ours.

Such friendships make a notable contribution to the cause of Anglo-American understanding. It is in the homes, not the hotels, of a nation that we each can learn the truth about our people.

Here I might make an appeal to those British business men who have dealings with the United States. When Americans call upon you over here, don't be content with purely business contacts. Ask them to your homes and your clubs, so that they may see something of the real England.

In these various ways the two great divisions of the English-speaking race may be drawn closer together.

Private contacts and friendships between individuals, by increasing the area of understanding and good will, pave the way for a closer understanding between the two nations and their governments, with all that this would mean to the peace of the world.

In spite of all impediments, Britain and America have never been closer in aim and purpose than now, or nearer to full mutual understanding.

Our ways have diverged in the past. I believe that, increasingly, they will lie together in the future.

We shall certainly follow the path of our joint destiny more prosperously, and far more safely, if we tread it together like good companions.

Anglo-American relations circa 1775: off to an unpromising start.

BOSTON MASSACRE.

Presidential Possibilities for '44

by Raymond Clapper

In 1943, Raymond Clapper, political journalist, took a look at Republican and New Deal Presidential hopefuls.

In politics, the big question is whether President Roosevelt will run for a fourth term. He is, without question, the dominant political figure, yet few would assume that he could be easily re-elected.

The uncertainties of politics are increased by the uncertainties of war. In wartime, people vote with far more explosive emotion than in peacetime. We saw how in the election last November even the most astute Republicans failed to realize how large a vote Republicans were to receive everywhere, a vote thrust upon them by a disgruntled electorate.

War is not only deep personal loss. It is also a mass of trivial irritations. The small irritations of today are the big anti-administration votes of tomorrow. Quick and easy victory in the last war did not save Woodrow Wilson and his administration from quick and overwhelming defeat immediately thereafter.

A President may win the war but may at the same time suffer retribution for the small inconveniences that were inevitable in the process of winning it. People may not turn against a President because he sent their sons to war. They are, however, liable to dislike him because they have had to restrict their automobile driving, fill out complicated forms, submit to food rationing, and undergo other irritating inconveniences. These are the little things that add up to furious popular indignation against an administration.

The political factions working against re-election of Mr. Roosevelt know that—and are counting upon it to help them when the time arrives.

Inside the Democratic Party, anti-New Deal Democrats are trying to capture the party. This is mainly the dream of Southern conservatives. They have willing allies in some Northern Democrats, led by Senator Wheeler, who are against Mr. Roosevelt because of past differences over either domestic or foreign policies. James A. Farley, deeply embittered, is spending a great deal of time working among local Democratic political leaders all around the country.

Jim Farley Anti–New Deal

If there is any chance of the Democratic Party being captured by these anti-Roosevelt forces, it lies in the political ability of Big Jim Farley. He took control of the New York State Democratic convention away from Mr. Roosevelt last fall. He nominated his own man, John J. Bennett, Jr., for governor against the President's open choice, Senator James M. Mead. Only in 1940, when Mr. Farley tried unsuccessfully to prevent the nomination of President Roosevelt for a third term, did his magic fail.

But he has won a new lease on life, as have all conservatives, from the last elections, and he is now drawing on his long experience and talents, and on his vast friendships among Democratic Party workers, to prevent the renomination of the President or the nomination of a Roosevelt-chosen successor. Mr. Farley himself is reported to have ambitions, as he openly had them in 1940. An attractive figure, widely loved, Jim lacks the depth and breadth for the times. He is more than a mere politician. Yet he has failed to show that he has the caliber of statesmanship called for in these times, although of course similar limitations have not always stood in the way of others.

I don't think any one can take the nomination away from Mr. Roosevelt if he wants to go after it. And I doubt that Mr. Roosevelt will retire, provided he feels able to carry the burden a while longer. There is growing recognition of the logic that if he remains in shape physically, he will be the best one to finish the war and initiate the peace. Some are clamoring for the President to declare his intentions now. In normal times that might be very desirable. I think it is too early to expect now a decision about a nomination that would be made a year from June.

The President's first choice, if he felt free and able to name a successor, undoubtedly would be Vice-President Wallace. He has indicated this in many ways. He has given Mr. Wallace important assignments in the war program. Mr. Wallace is far more than the figurehead that most Vice-Presidents become. But the choice of Mr. Wallace would not be unopposed even in innermost New Deal circles.

Paul McNutt, chairman of the War Manpower Commission, is not to be brushed aside if there is to be a new Democratic ticket. He built an effective organization in 1940; with wide support in the American Legion and among schoolteachers. His popularity among convention delegates in 1940 was demonstrated when a stampede in the convention tried to prevent him from withdrawing his name as a candidate for the Vice-Presidential nomination. However, his manpower task is a hard one that may cost him all of his past popularity.

Another possible New Deal figure is Associate Justice William O. Douglas. But not much can happen unless he is taken off the Supreme Court and given a more active assignment. He has many warm supporters, but his lack of experience in politics and the fact that he has never held elective office handicap them.

Clockwise from upper left are Presidential possibilities Thomas E. Dewey, Henry A. Wallace, William O. Douglas and Harold E. Stassen.

"Big Jim" Farley (Democratic National Chairman) wanted to unseat F.D.R.

Gov. Thomas Dewey: "I won't run."

Democratic conservatives have no available figures of national stature aside from James A. Farley. The nearest possibilities are Senators Byrd of Virginia and Tydings of Maryland. The conservatives may try to pick up a middle-of-the-road type. If James F. Byrnes survives his job as director of stabilization without making too many enemies, he might be advanced.

But Mr. Roosevelt will probably never abdicate to the conservative Democrats. His retreats are always slight—and strategic. In bringing Mr. Byrnes, a popular senator before he went to the Supreme Court, into the administration, Mr. Roosevelt was obviously making a gesture toward conservative elements in Congress. A similar motive may have dictated his appointment of Prentiss Brown to replace Leon Henderson as price administrator. Mr. Brown was a defeated Democratic senator from Michigan who had many contacts in Congress and was widely liked. Mr. Roosevelt often trims sail in face of danger. It does not indicate real retreat, but rather an ability to roll with the punch.

Generally speaking, it does not seem possible that the Democrats could win in 1944 with a conservative candidate. There are few conservatives of any national reputation and following among Democrats. If the past is any guide, it would be futile for the Democratic Party to go conservative. If a reaction is running toward Republicans, the tendency of the voters would be to elect a known conservative from the tried and true conservative party, instead of electing a Democratic conservative. That was demonstrated in 1924 when Democrats went into Wall Street and nominated John W. Davis out of the House of Morgan.

Willkie's Challenge

In the Republican Party, the controversy over Wendell Willkie is the central question. Primarily the controversy relates to a readjustment of the party's attitude toward foreign policy. There is a strong strain of isolationism in the Republican Party. It still is very much alive under the surface.

Mr. Willkie is the challenging personality in the Republican Party, the figure to be reckoned with. He made an excellent race against President Roosevelt in 1940, considering all of the circumstances. Yet regular party leaders have a strong distaste for him, which expresses itself privately in sharp language. But they are afraid of him. He still seems to have a large residue of popular support, brought over from the tremendous vote in 1940. He stands out for his color, his originality, his courage, his willingness to take a position that he feels is for the good of the country regardless of the traditional party line. His strength is indicated by the ganging-up against him among the regular machine politicians.

Some say that Mr. Willkie occupies a position in the Republican Party much like that so long occupied in the Democratic Party by William Jennings Bryan. Anyway, Mr. Willkie has a tremendous nuisance value, and whether or not the Republicans renominate him, he will not be ignored.

Governor Harold E. Stassen of Minnesota is a young and rapidly rising figure who has demonstrated the same courage and foresight regarding foreign policy that Mr. Willkie has

shown. In the supposedly isolationist state of Minnesota, he was re-elected for a third term last November, and on a platform advocating fullest participation by the United States in international affairs after the war. He is one of the most aggressive of the leaders who urge that the United Nations be transformed into a strong world organization after the war.

Stassen, Dewey, Bricker

Governor Stassen long ago decided to go into the navy as soon as his legislature adjourned. So for some time to come he will be out of politics, absent in uniform. He will have resigned as governor. Of course he expects to return to public life. He has friends who wish him to run for the Presidential nomination next year. The length of the war may have some bearing on his future plans. His youth gives him time.

Another young man is Governor Thomas Dewey of New York. He has the advantage of

Wendell Willkie tried, and failed, to oust Roosevelt in 1940.

having recently been elected governor of the President's own state. Because New York is the largest state, any man who can be elected governor there becomes an eligible Presidential figure unless specifically eliminated by some other consideration. And a Republican thus elected becomes of enormous interest as a vote-getting possibility.

However, Governor Dewey said at the time of his nomination for governor that he intended to devote himself wholly to the service of the people of New York for the next four years. He has repeated that statement several times since his election and has stated that he will not under any circumstances be a candidate for any nomination during his first term as governor. Neither politicians nor the people take such renunciations seriously. It is expected that Governor Dewey's attitude toward the nomination will depend entirely upon the outlook in the summer of 1944.

At the moment, the figure favored by a number of Republican Party insiders is Governor John W. Bricker of Ohio, a conservative who takes no stand on anything. Bricker has made a good governor of Ohio and has been re-elected for a third term by an unprecedented vote. He also carried Ohio in 1940 when President Roosevelt carried the state. Governor Bricker is a good Ohio vote getter.

Senator Robert A. Taft, twice the Presidential hope of Ohio Republicans, has stepped aside for Governor Bricker this time and has willed to him, at least for the time being, the Republican leaders in Southern states who form a nice nucleus at a national convention. Their allegiance to Taft, with a few exceptions, was demonstrated at the recent Republican National Committee meeting when a majority of the Southern national committee men and committee women supported his candidate for national chairman.

Governor Bricker is the current darling of the regular conservative party leaders who think that it will be politics as usual next year, with the same kind of set-up that the Republicans had when they shoved Harding into the sure-thing nomination of 1920. At that time the Republicans knew they would win, and the party insiders who knew what they wanted picked a nationally obscure and colorless candidate. If history is going to repeat, then it's Bricker by big odds.

GOP Wants National Hero

The first World War was the exception to the rule that wars produce a flock of Presidential candidates and some Presidents. Republicans are keeping their eyes open for a war hero. Already there has been much talk of General MacArthur, although apparently without any encouragement from him. It seems hardly likely that the war will be over by the summer of 1944, and that might obscure the attention that might otherwise be directed to Republican political figures now in uniform, such as Brigadier General Patrick Hurley, Brigadier General Theodore Roosevelt, Jr., and Brigadier General Hanford MacNider.

Thus Republicans have every type of prospective candidate. They have Willkie, the aggressive outspoken follower of the Roosevelt foreign policy; Stassen, the newer figure from the Middle West; Dewey, the passive vote getter in New York; Bricker, the silent favorite of the insiders; and several military figures.

Out of that list the Republicans will be able to pick a pair of candidates best adapted to the political conditions as they exist at the time of the campaign next year.

The unsinkable F.D.R. at his fourth inauguration.

The Political Effects of the War

by George Gallup

George Gallup, durable pollster, made a study in mid-1943 of the probable effects of the war on the 1944 elections.

Any one who thinks that prewar patterns of voting behavior will continue in the 1944 Presidential election will be in for a rude shock. The war has brought changes which are having a marked effect on politics and which may upset the best calculations of old-time political prophets.

While it would be an exaggeration, nevertheless one might say that the women and the old men will pick the next President.

Certainly they will have more to do with electing him than ever before in history.

The young men of the country will be absent from the voting booths. Somewhere between 7,000,000 and 11,000,000 of them will be in the armed forces by next year. Judging by the experience of the 1942 Congressional elections, it would be a miracle if many of them were to fill out absentee ballots. According to one estimate, only 2 per cent of the men in the armed forces voted in 1942. Unless some unprecedented move is made to change the situation, the number of soldier ballots is not expected to be large.

The absence of the young men at election time will hurt the Democrats more than the Republicans. The young age groups, particularly those under thirty, have always been pro-Roosevelt by about 60 per cent or more, and in recent surveys have shown no tendency to change their viewpoint. The bulk of the armed forces is made up of men under thirty. Hence, for every 100 soldiers who do not vote next year, the Democrats stand to lose about sixty votes, the Republicans only forty. That is a rough estimate only, but it illustrates one definite political effect of the war.

Women's Vote Largest

While the young men in the armed forces are taking care of the bullets, the women and the older men left at home will have to take care of the ballots. Relatively speaking, the situation places a greater political responsibility on the women of the country than they have ever chosen to exercise before.

The political attitudes of women during the last war were important, but they had less direct effect on elections because there was no woman suffrage at that time. The importance of the women's views today is indicated by the fact that last November, for the first time since woman suffrage, *more women went to the polls and voted than men.* In other years the women of the country cast not more than about 42 to 45 per cent of the total vote. Last November the female accounted for 53 per cent of the votes cast for congressmen, or a clear majority. The absence of men was the chief explanation, although women do take a more active interest in politics than they did a generation ago.

The higher ratio of women voting than men is likely to be maintained in 1944. Even if the war is over—which seems improbable—the men in service will not have been demobilized in sufficient numbers to affect the election very much.

The women's vote is going to be highly significant in 1944 because the women are a little more Republican than the men. At least, they were in the 1942 election. The difference is not great, but it could be important in a close election. A cross-section sampling check which embraced interviews in all forty-eight states with 14,000 people who voted in the last election shows that the women were 2.2 percentage points more Republican than the men. When that difference, small in itself, is projected into millions of votes, it is clear that the higher the proportion of votes cast by women next year, the more the Republicans stand to benefit.

More Older People

Also of aid to the G. O. P. will be the higher-than-normal ratio of older people in the voting population. All the elections of the last twelve years have shown that, outside the South, the older a voter is, the more Republican. This is shown in the following simple table. It gives the percentage of people by age groups who voted Republican in the Presidential election of 1940 and in the Congressional election of 1942. Note how the proportion voting Republican rises step by step as the age advances:

| | Per Cent Voting Republican | |
Age	1940	1942
21-29	40	46
30-49	44	50
50 and over	49	56

It is clear that Republican leaders would shed no tears if a larger part of the electorate were comprised of older people. Will that be the case in 1944? With the war on, all the evidence indicates that it will. It was definitely the case in 1942, when there were far fewer men in the Army than there will be next year. People over thirty years of age cast 88 per cent of the total vote for Congress in 1942, although they constitute only 80 per cent of the adult population, excluding the armed forces.

Conversely, the younger age groups, those between twenty-one and thirty, cast a disproportionately small share of the vote. They form one fifth of the adult population outside the armed forces, but they cast only one eighth of the vote in 1942.

Could Spell Difference

Republican advantage among women and older age groups might not be a decisive factor in a onesided election. But in a close election it could spell the difference between victory and defeat for the Democrats. It would be especially important in closely contested Congressional races in 1944.

Dr. George Gallup plans another Gallup Poll with his editorial and statistical staff.

Under the impact of war there is a growing movement to lower the voting age to eighteen. The argument is that if men are old enough to fight at eighteen, they are old enough to vote. Amendments to the state constitutions to lower the voting age have been introduced in thirteen states, and one state, Georgia, has already passed the measure, although final adoption awaits ratification by the people in August.

A lower voting age would have political implications which are not generally realized. So long as young voters remain pro-Democratic, as they are now, the Democrats have much more to gain by lowering the voting age than the Republicans. It would bring into the electorate more potential supporters for Roosevelt than for the G. O. P.

Once this fact is realized, it is likely that Democratic leaders will champion the lower voting age with much more enthusiasm than Republican leaders.

The most puzzling factor, the big question mark for 1944, is whether the war workers will turn out at the polls and vote. This applies especially to the migrant workers—the millions who pulled up stakes and moved to new communities to take war jobs both before and after Pearl Harbor. It is estimated that between 5,000,000 and 10,000,000 working people have shifted their place of work because of wartime conditions.

A large number of these migrant workers failed to vote in 1942, either because they could not fulfill residential qualifications for voting or because they did not take advantage of absentee balloting procedure. Among workers in war factories, for example, only about two in every five took the trouble to go to the polls, and that was one reason why the Democrats lost forty-eight seats in the House. Most skilled, semiskilled, and unskilled workers are Democrats.

Workers For Democrats

If the working class turns out in normal strength in 1944, it will be a terrific asset to the Democratic Party. If the workers stay home, it will seriously jeopardize the New Deal. It is no wonder that Democrats are as worried over absenteeism at the polls as industry is worried over absenteeism in the factories.

In the coming months we are bound to hear much talk among Democrats about getting workers to the polls. Labor unions are already becoming aware of the political implications of the worker-turnout problem in elections. The *New York Times* reported early in May that A. F. of L. leaders in Iowa have developed and approved a plan by which union dues would be increased five to ten cents a month, and the money used to pay bonuses to members if they vote on election day.

Democratic leaders can, of course, take cheer from the fact that the turnout in 1942 might not be typical of what is to happen in 1944. A midterm election nearly always produces a smaller turnout than a Presidential race. But it is noteworthy that the vote cast in 1942 (28,000,000) was the lightest in any election since the last war, and in terms of population one of the lightest in all history. There would have to be a prodigious increase to bring the total in 1944 back to the 50,000,000 votes cast in 1940.

It does not seem likely, however, that there will be any more major shifts of population in the next year or two to compare with those that have taken place in the last three. For that reason it would be logical to assume that the turnout of workers at the polls in 1944 will more nearly approximate normal than was the case last November. Institute studies show that the longer a person lives in a new community the more likely he is to vote.

A full turnout of war-industry workers will be an incalculable asset to the Democratic Party because from all present indications the workers are just as Democratic now as they were in 1940. One reason why President Roosevelt defeated Wilkie was that workers who are now employed in war industries voted Democratic by a 64-per-cent majority in that year. Had they turned out in full numbers in 1942 the Democrats would probably have lost few seats in the House. As for 1944, the present party preference among these workers is 69 per cent Democratic, according to the latest survey. In short, the New Deal, after twelve years in power, has to date retained most of its potent appeal to the working class—a fact which may explain the cautious attitude of the administration toward anti-union legislation.

It remains to be seen, of course, whether anti-

Roosevelt union leaders like John L. Lewis can influence their union followers into bolting the New Deal in 1944. According to present speculation, Lewis is out in dead earnest to beat Roosevelt next year by every means at his command. There is no question that Lewis wields great influence over labor where strictly union matters are concerned. But there is a grave question whether he wields the same influence over labor *politically*.

It will be remembered that in the closing days of the 1940 Presidential campaign, Lewis, to dramatize his opposition to Roosevelt, offered to resign as head of the C. I. O. if the President were re-elected. This move, if it was calculated to influence the rank and file of C. I. O. members into voting against the New Deal, brought notoriously poor results. In a check-up after the election, the Institute found through a survey that C. I. O. members actually gave Roosevelt a higher proportion of their votes than did members of the A. F. of L., whose leaders had been pro-Roosevelt all along! It is a favorite delusion in American politics that one man can "deliver" a nation-wide bloc of votes to any party he chooses. American voters seldom behave in such sheeplike fashion.

Another reason why a full labor turnout next year is so important to the Democrats is that their prospects are far less favorable than usual along the farm front. Farm defection from the New Deal, which began as early as the election of 1936, was accelerated in 1940 and 1942. An examination of the farm vote shows that whereas farmers were Democratic in 1936 by 59 per cent and in 1940 by 54 per cent, those who cast ballots in the 1942 Congressional races voted only 42 per cent Democratic.

Roosevelt was, of course, not on the ticket in 1942, and for that reason the farm vote last November probably does not adequately foreshadow what will happen next year if Roosevelt runs. Nevertheless, it seems likely that Republicans can count on greater farm support next year than ever before. That fact only emphasizes again the importance to the Democrats of getting out the labor vote—in order to offset losses in the farm areas.

What About Fourth Term?

What is the country's attitude toward a Roosevelt fourth term? With the nominating conventions still just about a year away, the public has pretty well made up its mind that Mr. Roosevelt will be a candidate. Six out of every ten voters with opinions on the subject, polls find, think he will run, and an even larger proportion are convinced that he will run if the war is still on.

Although much will depend on how strong a candidate the Republicans pick, the war seems to be the biggest factor in the President's chances for re-election. The Institute recently completed a survey in which it asked people (1) whether they would vote for Roosevelt for a fourth term if the war is over, and (2) how they would vote if the war is still going on. The results indicate that sentiment for a fourth term would run twelve percentage points higher if the war is still in progress. That margin could make the difference between victory and defeat. The results were: (1) if the war is over—39 per cent for Roosevelt, 50 per cent against, 11 per cent undecided; (2) if the war is still going on—51 per cent for Roosevelt, 37 per cent against, 12 per cent undecided.

Dr. Gallup checks tabulated poll results.

There is no doubt that the fourth-term issue will cost Mr. Roosevelt some votes if he runs, just as the third-term issue did in 1940. But in 1940 the third term was not the deciding factor. The most important factor was the war situation, which the public thought Mr. Roosevelt could handle better than Wendell Wilkie. By the same token it is likely that the war, rather than the fourth-term question, will be the determining factor in 1944.

But at this distance from the election there is every indication that the 1944 race will be close.

If we look at the situation purely on the basis of the last election, the indicated division of electoral votes at that time is extremely close. It can be figured by using the 1942 Congressional election returns for each state and making allowance for the relation between the vote for Congress and the vote for President that existed in 1940.

This shows an electoral vote lineup having all the elements of a horse race, as follows: Republicans, 290 electoral votes; Democratic, 241. It takes 266 to elect.

However, the President was not on the ticket last November.

If we look at the situation in terms of "trial heats" between specific candidates, there is also evidence of a close race. In one of these trial heats the Institute recently matched a Democratic ticket of Roosevelt and Wallace against a Republican ticket of Thomas E. Dewey for President and General Douglas MacArthur for Vice-President, and asked people throughout the country how they would vote.

The result came out 54 per cent for Roosevelt-Wallace, 46 per cent for Dewey-MacArthur.

It should be remembered that, because of the surplus Democratic majorities in the South, a Democratic candidate for President needs to poll a minimum of around 52 per cent of the popular vote in order to win in the electoral college. In 1888 Grover Cleveland, a Democrat, polled 50.4 per cent of the popular vote—a majority—yet he lost in the electoral vote.

FDR Leads Democrats

There seems little doubt that President Roosevelt is the outstanding choice for the nomination among Democratic voters. In May a survey found him polling nearly four times more than the combined vote for six other possible Democratic candidates. The President was the choice of 79 per cent of Democrats in this survey, with Henry Wallace next with 8 per cent, and James A. Farley next with 5 per cent.

In the ranks of Republican voters, on the other hand, no such one-sided attitude prevails concerning possible G. O. P. nominees for the Presidency.

Governor Dewey of New York, Wendell L. Willkie, General MacArthur, and Governor Bricker of Ohio are the most popular choices of the rank and file, but none of these four commands a majority at this time.

When Republican voters in a survey were handed a list of seven men who have been mentioned most frequently in political circles as possible G. O. P. Presidential material, and asked to state their choice, the results were as follows:

	Per Cent
Dewey	38
Willkie	28
MacArthur	17
Bricker	8
Stassen	7
Saltonstall	1
Warren	1

As every one knows, Presidential nominees are picked by convention delegates and not by the rank and file of the parties. Sometimes the delegates follow the sentiment of the rank and file and sometimes they do not.

In conservative Republican circles there is much talk of Governor Bricker as the next G. O. P. candidate. From the above table it can be seen that he is not well known throughout the rank and file of the party at the present time, although other surveys have found that voters who know him look upon him favorably.

Is it an advantage or a disadvantage to a candidate to hold a popular lead this far away from convention time?

That question is being widely discussed in Republican circles. The political history of the past twenty-five years tends to substantiate the argument that it is an advantage, rather than a disadvantage, to hold an early popular lead. In the majority of cases the conventions have picked men who had outstanding popular support for many months before convention time. In the last three elections Mr. Willkie was the only exception.

Labor May Be Problem

No matter whom the Republicans pick next year, one of the big problems of the party is going to be its labor platform. An outstanding opportunity lies open to capitalize on the rising public resentment of labor-union practices—a resentment constantly fanned by wartime strikes. At the same time the G. O. P. is naturally fearful of alienating possible labor support at the polls through adopting too strong a platform for union control.

Is there a way out of the dilemma? From a recent Institute survey comes a possible clue. This study found that there is overwhelming sentiment both on the part of the general public *and on the part of labor-union members* for legislation to require unions to report the money they take in and spend. Union members want to know what becomes of their dues money just as much as the public does. A platform plank advocating such legislation, while it would appeal to the public as a step toward union regulation, might at the same time find considerable support from the rank and file of labor. It is a way out of the Republican dilemma.

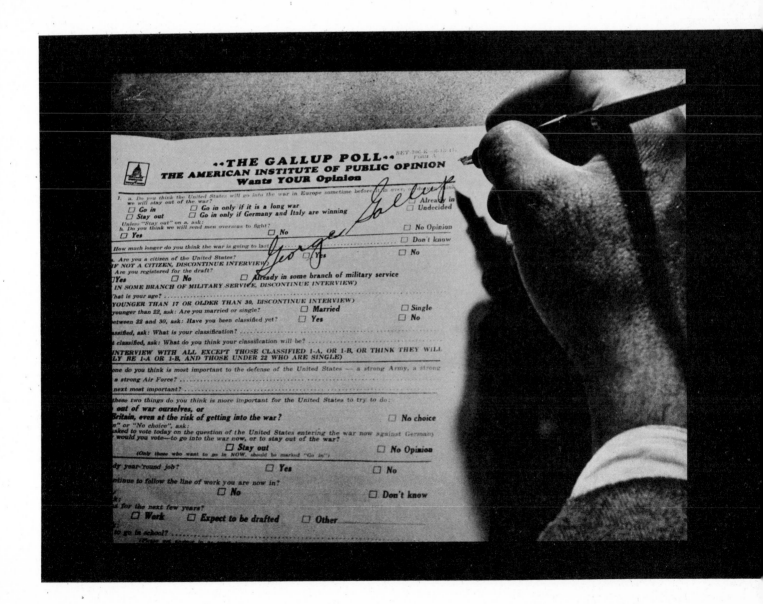

The Charter of the United Nations

by Paul Hunter

Paul Hunter in 1945 looked at the weaknesses of the U.N. Charter as well as its strengths.

Like all human documents, the Charter of United Nations produced at San Francisco will function well or badly according to the caliber of men who through the years are entrusted with power in their respective nations, particularly the "Big Five."

The Charter does not give the world an airtight guaranty against future aggression of war. It will still be possible, though a little more difficult, for a future Führer of one of the Big Five to imbue his people with the idea they are a superior folk who have been robbed of rights and honors which the Almighty intended for them. It will still be possible for a lesser nation, aided and abetted by one of the Big Five, to do likewise.

It was in this manner the peace of the world was broken and World War II came about. If, among any of the Big Five, such a man should rise to power, and if his people are fools enough to fight and die at his behest, the peace of the world will be broken once more.

We had best not delude ourselves that anything in the United Nations Charter will prevent it.

The so-called freedom-of-discussion provision of the Charter can do no more than bring the moral force of the world opinion to bear against an aggressor. There was plenty of discussion and ample moral force marshaled against Japan, Italy, and Germany in the old League of Nations, but these aggressors paid little attention to it.

The basic weakness of the Charter is that it does not define categorically just what physical, economic, or diplomatic acts constitute aggression. Thus, if a disturber of the peace does arise, he can argue endlessly that his aggressions are not aggression. Like Hitler, he can claim that what looks like aggression is only self-defense and no one can call him a liar by the book. The United Nations must then either pretend such aggression doesn't exist, or the war will be on, with the various nations lining up for or against the aggressor according to what they conceive to be their interests.

Nevertheless, the accomplishments of San Francisco are notable in the world's history. A wide area of agreement has been reached covering much of the world's affairs. Last but not least, the meeting has produced the recognition by the United States that it is part of the world and has assured the world we intend to play our part. Doubt on this point encouraged aggression before. Removal of the doubt will do much to discourage it in the future.

Though not perfect, the Charter is a good charter and has within it the seeds of permanent peace, provided the people of the world make their desire for peace prevail and place their destinies always in the hands of men of good will.

No charter, not even a perfect one, could keep the peace if sinister men bent on making war are placed in positions where they can do so.

Historic moment: U.S. Senator Tom Connally signs United Nations Charter. June 26, 1945. President Truman is at far left.

THE CHARTER OF THE UNITED NATIONS

PREAMBLE

WE THE PEOPLES OF THE UNITED NATIONS

determined to save succeeding generations from the scourge of war, which twice in our lifetime has brought untold sorrow to mankind, and

to reaffirm faith in fundamental human rights, in the dignity and value of the human person, in the equal rights of men and women and of nations large and small, and

to establish conditions under which justice and respect for the obligations arising from treaties and other sources of international law can be maintained, and

to promote social progress and better standards of life in larger freedom,

and for these ends

to practice tolerance and live together in peace with one another as good neighbors, and

to unite our strength to maintain international peace and security, and

by the acceptance of principles and the institution of methods, to insure that armed force shall not be used, save in the common interest, and

by the employment of international machinery for the promotion of economic and social advancement of all peoples,

have resolved to combine our efforts to accomplish these aims.

Accordingly, our respective governments, through representatives assembled in the City of San Francisco, who have exhibited their full powers found to be in good and due form, have agreed to the present Charter of the United Nations and do hereby establish an international organization to be known as the United Nations.

Roosevelt–Man and Statesman

by Jonathan Daniels

Jonathan Daniels, the son of Wilson's Secretary of the Navy, was an administrative assistant to FDR. He wrote this appraisal in 1945.

History, being written generally by men with neat minds, will undoubtedly divide the twelve years of Franklin D. Roosevelt into the two periods of war and peace—war and reform. In a sense, he himself once so divided it in one of the lighthearted parables in which he liked to dress serious concerns.

He spoke of two entirely different gentlemen: Old Doc New Deal and Dr. Win-the-War. I doubt that there were any such different doctors. Indeed, I believe that there was only one doctor, only one disease, and that in the whole twelve years the one remedy steadily applied was a determination to make democracy effective for the security and in the defense of free men. It worked almost to scientific demonstration that there are no limits to the powers and the possibilities of democracy gallantly led and confidently following.

Certainly only a person precise to the point of insanity would date the war service of President Roosevelt from 1.47 P. M. EWT, December 7, 1941. Then he received the first news almost accidentally, in a picked-up message of first alarm to naval personnel in Hawaiian waters, that the Japs were bombing Pearl Harbor. No sensible person had talked with a true sense of security in peace since Hitler marched into Poland in September, 1939. It was a strange item in history that Hitler, who believed in stars, came into power just five weeks before Franklin Roosevelt and on Franklin Roosevelt's birthday. The stars may not have been fixed, but tragedy and destiny already had fallen into shape for mankind.

Twelve years later it somehow seems more than a coincidence that Roosevelt died in April, as Lincoln died. The lilacs of the Lincoln legend were in bloom again. When Lincoln fell, Lee had surrendered; but a mourning nation had to wait eleven days beyond his death before Johnston ended his fighting with Sherman. Roosevelt saw the Americans across the Rhine. All that remained for victory in Europe were the signed and dated documents for the "unconditional surrender" he had demanded. The proclamation of victory which his successor read on May 8 had already been written before Roosevelt died.

American carriers, built under Roosevelt's devoted direction of the Navy, had stood in the roadsteads less than fifty miles off Tokyo and sent their planes with implacably increasing destruction upon the Japs. Iwo Jima had fallen. Okinawa had been invaded. In the rubble of Berlin, Adolf Hitler survived. But he survived only as the malefactor condemned by the American who paralleled his period and prevented by effective democratic leadership his fulfillment of purpose against human freedom.

It was a triumphant time for a great man to die. And it was clear, before the bugles sounded last inside the hemlock hedges at Hyde Park, that he was not merely a great man dead, but that he stood already as the symbol of the American destiny in his time.

Better than any other man he understood that destiny. He was no solemn statesman in a plug hat. He had been wearing a pull-over sweater when he began his confident direction of the war as Commander in Chief on Pearl Harbor Sunday. Afterward war workers and soldiers, sailors and statesmen saw him in a flannel shirt, old hat, and casually knotted bow tie. He was a shirt-sleeves man in an informal America and he spoke its language to its under-

Roosevelt, Gen. Charles De Gaulle (second from right), and Winston Churchill at Casablanca, 1943.

The "Big Three": Churchill, Roosevelt, and Stalin at Yalta, 1945.

Winston Churchill at Christmas services with the Roosevelts in Washington, 1941.

standing in great matters and small. And because he believed in the dignity of the American, he was never afraid to ask or expect America's courage.

He was speaking of war in the world and democracy at home as two inseparable parts of his work and his time, in 1936 at Philadelphia when he declared that this generation of Americans had a rendezvous with destiny. He repeated it in January, 1939, when the imminence of war was obvious to all but the most blind of those Americans who sought to exorcise war by denying its danger.

"Once I prophesied," he told the Congress, "that this generation of Americans had a ren-

dezvous with destiny. That prophecy comes true. To us much is given; more is expected.

"This generation will nobly save or meanly lose the last best hope of earth."

When he died, the chance of salvation was certain, but certain only because of the great burdens he had seemed almost gaily to bear until the day he died under the long weariness of his load.

Belabored And Beloved

It is difficult to remember any great American who was so belabored in his lifetime and so beloved by so many at the same time. He did not come to the storm of war from a cloudless America. The fighting at home continued straight up to the war—and beyond it. But it was the same fighting for Roosevelt. He believed that democracy must be effective to survive.

It was no accident that he chose the occasion of the dedication of a bridge, one of the public works built by his administration for the peaceful convenience of a creative people, for his famous Quarantine Speech in Chicago on October 5, 1937. He did not mention Doc New Deal or Dr. Win-the-War then, but he did use the metaphor of medicine when he spoke of the plague of international lawlessness already apparent in the world. It did not please the dictators. Some Americans did not like it. But he made clear his warning that if the disease were permitted to spread, "let no one imagine that America would escape."

He understood that warning as the man first responsible for its meaning in America. He was grim as he spoke it—grim as he could be,

with his great shoulders forward, his eyes hard blue. He looked young still. He was fifty-five, in vigorous middle life, son of a mother still living at eighty-three and a father who had lived to be seventy-two. The paralysis which had steeled his mind seemed to have strengthened his body also. He seemed even a bigger man above his useless legs.

Isolationism Forgotten

He had reason to be confident. The year before, he had received the greatest vote any President had ever received in a contested election. No President had ever come to the White House in the midst of such domestic crisis as he did, save only Lincoln. In four years he had given America long pent-up and long blindly resisted social and economic safeguards essential to the vitality of its democracy. True enough, he had been halted in some of his plans; not every reform had worked perfectly, but he had won the overwhelming confidence

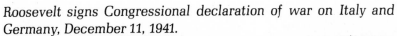

Roosevelt signs Congressional declaration of war on Italy and Germany, December 11, 1941.

of people who wanted democracy to work. There were more fights to make for them. Then, at fifty-five, in the fullness of his powers and the powers of America for its people, he knew that forces grew in ruthlessness whose patent purpose was to see democracy destroyed.

It is a very easy thing to note now that the war began less than two years later. It is less easy to remember those ghostly symbols of world security, the Maginot Line, the French Army, the strange powers attributed to and expected from the British Fleet. In terms of the crackpots who have persisted, it is not easy to recall the respectability of rigid isolationism in the years before the war—and after it, before Pearl Harbor. Not many people remember that in the summer before Hitler marched into Poland the Congress declined to modify the Neutrality Act of 1935 which bound the President's hands and made it impossible for American industrial power to stand with the French Army and the British Fleet as potentials against German aggression.

Destroyers And Draft

Roosevelt hoped for peace for America, but he did not mean that America should idly allow the dictatorships to destroy the democracies. When war came, he made a point of describing the peculiar quality of our neutrality by his statement that "even a neutral has a right to take account of facts. Even a neutral cannot be asked to close his mind or his conscience." He moved immediately—and successfully this time—to secure such change in the Neutrality Act as would make it possible for American industry to supply French and British fighting forces. It was "cash and carry" then, but only the Allies could come and get it.

Some historians given to labels have called America's part before Pearl Harbor America's "soft" war. After the fall of France, it became quickly tougher in Presidential utterance as well as Presidential act. The whole surplus store of American arms went by fast freighters to a Britain left unarmed after Dunkirk. By

No Peace on Earth: The Roosevelts and Churchill enroute to 1941 Christmas services a few short weeks after U.S. entered WW II.

September the President had found a way to let Britain have fifty destroyers in a deal for bases in this hemisphere. Already, then, war production in the United States was growing to the possibility of the President's invention of the great American war weapon of lend-lease.

In September also—and in the midst of a national election campaign—he secured the Selective Training and Service Act providing the first draft of men in peacetime in American history. In peacetime, too, he secured the right to seize industrial plants not co-operating on defense orders. Camps grew, ships rose on the ways, new American fleets took the seas. Production began to answer the incredulity that had greeted the President's goal of 50,000 planes. In the archives in Washington there are memos bearing the scrawl of approval and injunction, "Work Fast—FDR."

FDR In Command

The Japanese solved the problem of American isolation. And solved it on a Sunday afternoon while the President, relaxing for a little in the oval study at the White House and nursing the sinuses that plagued him all his life, was working at his stamp book. Before he went late to bed, almost every major participant in the "defense" effort had been with him on the first day of war. The attack, which had come under the mask of negotiations still under way in Washington when the bombs dropped, was surprise and naval disaster, but it found Washington in full stride of preparation for the greatest war ever undertaken.

That day the Commander in Chief gave orders like a commander on the bridge of a ship. One who watched him work has spoken of his "genius in disorder" and said that his command on that crowded seventh of December was to be compared only with his confident leadership on his first days in the White House when the national economy seemed tottering. The crowds which had heard the news gathered outside the White House fence. The Cabinet members, the generals, and the admirals came in. They found a leadership which did not relax while he lived.

Nobody knows yet how to count or measure such a war. The greatest war we had ever fought before was concerned with only a single European land front and the Atlantic Ocean. Roosevelt's leadership in this war concerned men on every continent and every sea. In what we had called the World War before, we were engaged for only nineteen months, and only for part of that time were large American forces engaged. This war began with men dying, and the fighting had gone on for three years and five months when Roosevelt died.

In this war, lend-lease to our allies alone has cost more in dollars than our total spending before. For this war American industrial production is more than three times as great as in 1918 and nearly half of the total national production has been for war purposes, a proportion twice as great as that in the peak year of the last war. The arsenal of democracy was working as the arsenal of destruction.

Darkness To Victory

All this production and power and treasure was to be under the direction of one man. He took the direction and held it. He called tough old Admiral William D. Leahy to the White House as his personal chief of staff and through him kept in close touch with both the joint (U. S.) Chiefs of Staff and the combined (Anglo-American) Chiefs of Staff. On the ground floor of the White House a specially guarded and staffed map room was set up where messages were received about the progress of our forces

Roosevelt holds resolutions which put U.S. at war with Italy and Germany.

everywhere. On the maps he watched the war of men and supplies, of strategy and logistics, of heroism and death and victory.

It was a dark story at first—Guam and Wake and Midway and Bataan. Then slowly the men and production and ships and planes which were his concern became his concern also in Coral Sea, Midway again, Komandorskie Straits, Guadalcanal, Attu, Kiska, Bougainville, Tarawa, Kwajalein, Eniwetok, Hollandia, Saipan, Guam again, the Palaus and Leyte, on toward Japan. The first great secret enterprise came at last to other maps: Casablanca, Oran, Algiers, Tunis, Kasserine Pass, and on to Gela, Salerno, Messina, bloody Anzio, tough Cassino, to Rome. Rome somehow seemed the signal for the greatest secret and toughest job of all, Normandy. The President had been sick, but he was gay that June day.

"What are you fellows grinning about?" he wanted to know, grinning wide and happy himself.

Within five months the Americans alone sent more fighting men to France—men fully equipped—than the entire expeditionary force of the last war. And yet, within the same period

at the other side of the world, we landed a force sufficient to ensure the liberation of the Philippines. We were clearly already on the victory road.

Under Roosevelt's direction we built a Navy greater than the combined navies of all our allies and enemies. No greater Army ever marched under the American flag, or in equipment and quality under any other. The air power we built broke Germany and shatters Japan. These are the parts of victory certainly, but only a part of the evidence of leadership which Roosevelt provided in this war. In the faith he created among the three great Allies and all the United Nations, he was a force for victory in himself.

Stalin And Churchill

A whole decade before he met the monolithic Stalin in Teheran, he had extended the first hand of recognition to the almost pariah Russians in 1933. Our full safety and solidarity in the Western Hemisphere grew straight from the Good Neighbor policy and its observance, which proved not merely to the Americans but also to the world our international good in-

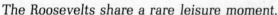

The Roosevelts share a rare leisure moment.

tentions. Roosevelt's ardent and early aid to Britain made the simplest Briton as well as its first statesman regard him as a friend. In a whole world in trouble he seemed the man men everywhere believed they could trust.

Such faith is not to be counted in terms of divisions or battleships. It meant much at home in terms of production. He was a man as well as a commander to our fighting men. In America his train moved to war plants and military camps. His friendship for Churchill, formally begun on the foggy seas of the Newfoundland bight where they bound their purpose to freedom in the Atlantic Charter, was a good affection warmed by many meetings. The President was not bothered by Churchill's occasional intellectual arrogance. He was not unduly impressed on a visit to his Maryland hideaway when Churchill recited the whole of Barbara Frietchie and then turned in casual erudition to the nonsense verse of Edward Lear. He was sometimes amused by Churchill's Tory fears. I had a feeling, as he talked of him, that he liked to bait him a little, even to tease him in the dead-pan presence of Stalin, who, he discovered, could laugh. The President had a deep respect for Stalin. I remember once his speaking of a plan for the solution of some problem he had outlined to the Marshal. He mimicked Stalin's brief, decisive thoughtfulness.

"I had not thought of it," he quoted the Marshal as saying. "It is a good idea. I will sign."

And that was that. It was very different with Churchill at that time. Describing him and imitating him, the President put his hands up defensively. "Churchill is acting now as if he is always afraid of getting hit."

Last Conference

The nature of the differences of the Marshal and the Prime Minister placed Roosevelt between them. In the deepest sense he had the trust of both. It was not accident that at Yalta, by general consent, he served as the chairman of the last great conference of his life.

There can have been few greater moments in history than that time at Yalta. Victory in Europe was clearly before them. They reached decisions which the happiness of the world cannot allow to disintegrate. It was a great time— and a happy one as well.

But it was not a happy voyage home. Before the cruiser Quincy turned toward home they knew that "Pa" Watson was dying. General Edwin Watson was a good deal more than the President's secretary and military aide. He was an arm upon whom the President literally leaned when he undertook to walk in his steel braces. More than anybody else, perhaps, he was the President's "tonic." It was his job to protect the President from overlong and overtalkative appointments. It was his gift and grace that he had warmth and charm and great good laughter. Also, he loved the President very much. And somewhere between Gibraltar and the Azores he died—of a cerebral hemorrhage.

The President came home to the piled mass of the details of his leadership which included more work and worry than exaltation. His report on Yalta was received with acclaim. But there were complaints on the home front. There was politics still. Politics had never abated for one moment. When it was worst it pretended to a greater patriotism than the President's. Fortunately, sometimes it amused him. Indeed, nothing seemed as eternal about him as his full-bodied laughter. It was one of the qualities which made him seem almost a man designed by nature to survive the strain of the American Presidency in such a war as this.

"Like A Fat Cherub"

His gaiety was like Lincoln's humor—the releasing levity of a deeply serious man. Certainly as he grew older and more weary, he was not the debonair Roosevelt of the first crowded days in the White House. But he seemed in conversation still the self-confident, laughing, sometimes outrageous Roosevelt who used humor as a tool and a weapon and a release. It was not the humor of an easygoing man. It could arm indignation, as he showed, a year before he died, in his famous speech to the Teamsters. Humor was a part of his famous characteristic of reducing the most serious things to simplicity: Lend-lease was a garden hose lent to a neighbor whose house was on fire.

He loved to tell the story of the origin of the name "United Nations" during Churchill's first swift visit to Washington after Pearl Harbor. They had struggled over combinations of fine words for a name for their league of belligerents. None of them seemed satisfactory. "United Nations" came to F. D. R. at night. Next morning he rolled into Churchill's bedroom. The Prime Minister was bathing. The President waited, and Churchill came out of the bathroom without a stitch of clothing on.

"He looked like a fat cherub," the President recalled.

But that morning he said, "Winston, I have found the name, 'United Nations.'"

The naked Churchill considered it solemnly and gave it his approval. Only after he had indicated his agreement did he seem to be aware of his nakedness.

"Later," said the President, "he told the King about it: 'Your Majesty, you are the only King of England whose Prime Minister has been received by the Chief of a State while completely nude.'"

FDR--Collector

Some people with neat little minds sometimes found the easy ranging mind of Roosevelt disorderly. They were shocked by his humorous memories of solemn occasions. It could, of course, be disconcerting to call about a job and spend your time talking stamps, or the venereal disease rate in Liberia, or a plan for the reforestation of the shores of the Persian Gulf. Conversation could be a defense with him as laughter was. But he could, in the first years of the war, turn easily in diversion for its own sake.

Much will be written about his collection of books, stamps, prints. His greatest collecting was not tangible: Everywhere he went—Casablanca, Teheran, Yalta even—he collected an amazing amount of non-essential but lively details about life and people. His interest in geography was never limited to maps. He even collected such evanescent things as bird calls. I know that during the earliest and most jittery days of the war he disturbed the Secret Service detail by a strange postmidnight sortie. His companions were some learned ornithologists who had come to join him in a contest as to which of them could identify the greatest number of night sounds made by Dutchess County birds. He was proud of his long-standing membership in the Union of Ornithologists, but enjoyed claiming that that membership had

greatly befuddled investigators of the Dies Committee when they were looking for left-wing organizations. "They couldn't tell," he said, "whether it was A. F. of L. or C. I. O."

Parables And Proverbs

He collected also, or invented—for private conversation and for his speaking to millions —parables to show his problems and make his points. And there was the proverb he brought back from Casablanca for those New Dealers, old friends and supporters, who had grown more worried as the war went on. They became very worried about American dealings in the conquest of North Africa with the Vichy French. I think he had been waiting a long time to give them his precise answer.

The President had faith in people as well as affection for them, but he was a realist about people also. Sometimes he was too kind to people upon whose affection and loyalty he knew he could depend even though their abilities were limited. Also, he used some people who were simple enough to think they were using him. He did not feel called upon to explain himself to his friends. He himself was confident of his goals. He attributed the proverb which he brought back from Casablanca to one of the Balkan countries, but it always sounded pure Roosevelt to me:

"In time of trouble, my children, it is given to you that you may go with the devil as far as the bridge."

Essential Rights

He never would have asked for patience directly, but the request was there. He had a war to fight. Nothing seemed to him so important as winning it with the least loss of American lives and in such a way as to assure the continuance of democracy in security for all Americans. Somehow nobody ever seemed to recall he had four boys in that war—none of them in safety zones. For them, for other Americans, for himself, victory meant making democracy work for men, women, and children. The steps he took in building power for war were accompanied all the way by the clearest insistence upon the purpose of the war as the protection and fulfillment of the possibilities of democracy. That insistence was the essence of the Four Freedoms attached to the lend-

TO THE CONGRESS OF THE UNITED STATES:

On the morning of December eleventh, the Government of Germany, pursuing its course of world conquest, declared war against the United States.

The long known and the long expected has thus taken place. The forces endeavoring to enslave the entire world now are moving towards this hemisphere.

Never before has there been a greater challenge to life, liberty, and civilization.

Delay invites greater danger. Rapid and united effort by all of the peoples of the world who are determined to remain free will ensure a world victory of the forces of justice and of righteousness over the forces of savagery and of barbarism.

Italy also has declared war against the United States.

I therefore request the Congress to recognize a state of war between the United States and Germany, and between the United States and Italy.

Franklin D. Roosevelt

THE WHITE HOUSE,

December 11, 1941.

lease proposal of 1941. The same essential freedoms were fixed in the fighting purposes of Britain and America in the Atlantic Charter in 1941. In 1944 he advanced from freedoms to rights in the economic bill of rights which he embodied in his January message to Congress on the state of the Union. He repeated that bill of rights in his speech at Soldier Field at Chicago in October. It is worth remembering now:

The right of a useful and remunerative job in the industries, or shops, or farms, or mines of the nation;

The right to earn enough to provide adequate food and clothing and recreation;

The right of every farmer to raise and sell his products at a return which will give him and his family a decent living;

The right of every business man, large and small, to trade in an atmosphere of freedom from unfair competition and domination by monopolies at home and abroad;

The right of every family to a decent home;

The right to adequate medical care and the opportunity to achieve and enjoy good health;

The right to adequate protection from the economic fears of old age, sickness, accident, and unemployment;

The right to a good education.

War Made Him Old

"All these rights," the President said, "spell security. And after this war is won we must be prepared to move forward, in the implementation of these rights, to new goals of human happiness and well-being."

He understood the opposition to such ideals. He knew better than most Americans that there were men who regarded the war as a new phase, a new turning to the right—away from the program he and the great mass of Americans who had four times elected him had worked out together.

Just a week before he died he wrote again his determination and his faith to an old political friend:

". . . I am sure that Americans who have done so much in the winning of the war have no doubt that we can give victory the rich meaning of full employment in the United States and of assistance to other nations in their reconstruction. Victory, without the use for

abundance of the powers we have developed in production for war, would be, indeed, a hollow victory. We must plan security and abundance together. Such a stronger American economy will be essential to carry out the responsibilities that lie in plans made at Bretton Woods, Hot Springs, and Dumbarton Oaks. Similarly, abundance at home depends upon organization for order and security in the world."

He was tired then, but not changed. He understood the American destiny of which he had been both the prophet and the leader. It had not altered. But, better than anybody else, he knew how weary he was, how suddenly, quickly, the war had made him old. He could see the wavering signature where so recently the bold scrawl had been. He was not fooled. But others were—some who loved him most. The spark of humor and liveliness never left his face, and somehow I think that misled his friends, as people who saw only the photographed image were not misled.

Died Right For History

Well, perhaps he died right for history. We can say that easily, remembering the abortive tragedy of Wilson, who had no historic right to live after he was stricken at Wichita. He not only failed to get peace; he lingered in its dissolution. Somehow there seems no tragedy now about Lincoln's dying. He departed in fitness with victory. But we forget much about Lincoln; we remember the funeral train and Walt Whitman's lilacs and forget that death interrupted his devotion to freedom for people. And peace and people made the joint heritage Roosevelt left us. He knew that peace and freedom are inseparable and that there can be no enduring peace except upon a decent earth.

We shall have to wait to know his full greatness—and our own.

The U.S. entered the World War at 4:10 P.M., December 8, 1941, with the signing of declaration of war against Japan.

The Most Powerful Man in America

by Harold L. Ickes

Harold Ickes, Roosevelt's tough outspoken Secretary of the Interior, in 1946 wrote about the tough boss of the United Mine Workers, John L. Lewis.

The most powerful man in the country today, and not the least dictatorial-minded, is John L. Lewis, the scowling president of the United Mine Workers of America. He has held that prominence since the end of the war, and as a matter of fact, had it not been for the Japanese attack on Pearl Harbor, he would have become the most powerful man in the country on December 7, 1941.

If this seems to be a strong statement, consider what Mr. Lewis can do, if he so desires. He can shut down the nation's steel mills, halt the production of automobiles, black out half of the cities of America, bring most of the railroads to a standstill, shut off the heat in 10,000,000 homes, throw millions out of work, directly or secondarily, and, among other things, end the production of nylons, thus blighting the lives of American women.

Practically all our railroads burn coal. Much of our electricity is produced in steam-driven plants. Most of our homes, whether they be single dwellings or apartments, are heated by coal. It is the basic ingredient out of which nylon, plastics, and important synthetic drugs such as the sulfa family are manufactured. The plain fact is that this country operates by coal.

For all practical purposes, there is little or no coal in this country which is produced unless by the grace of John L. Lewis.

This situation has been true ever since Pearl Harbor day, for it was on that day that John L. Lewis signed a contract which brought into the United Mine Workers union the last important group of unorganized employees in the coal mining industry—the miners who worked for the steel companies in the so-called "captive mines."

By this contract Lewis achieved a virtual monopoly over the labor of almost all of those who work in the coal mines. Had not the war intervened, thereby increasing tremendously the powers of President Roosevelt, Lewis might well have become the country's economic dictator.

Controls As Dictator

His strength lies not only in the fact that the miners of his union produce almost all of the bituminous and anthracite mined in the United States, but in his dictatorial control of that union, and the nature of coal mining.

Since he assumed the presidency of the union, he has controlled it through the power of union patronage. He exercises arbitrarily the power to appoint and to pay out of the union treasury all of the organizers of the mine workers and many of the union officials, and these appointments are not subject to review. In short, there has not been, nor is there now, much democracy in the mine workers' union. Like other dictators, Lewis has grown more powerful by the jealous use of his power. He not only holds and exercises the appointing power of the union; he is the custodian of its funds out of which he pays salaries and emoluments determined only by himself. In the depths of the depression the only people in the mine workers' organization who were making a decent living were the organizers and district officials. Is it any wonder that they were loyal to John L. Lewis, the man who could hire them at a salary determined by himself—and fire them?

In some districts a residual degree of autonomy and democracy was retained and the district president elected. But whenever a president has been selected in opposition to the wishes of Lewis, or when one elected with the approval of Lewis came to disagree with the great man, the district was likely to be invaded by scores of organizers from the national headquarters—"goon squads" the miners call them. And that would be the end of the recalcitrant president. To put it another way, Lewis uses the funds of the union workers to keep them in servile, or at least in uncomfortable, submission to himself.

What helps to make the mine workers' union an almost unbreakable monopoly is the fact that, as Lewis said, "You cannot mine coal with bayonets"—even during a war. Not even Hitler was able to mine coal with bayonets at the height of the Nazi power. In the countries which the Nazis overran, the miners were kept in the pits not so much by bayonets as by food rations and wages that were much larger than those given other residents of the occupied countries, and by allowing the miners to walk off with coal to sell on the black market.

What Kind Of Man?

The importance of the working miner, and hence of the man who controls him, lies in the fact that mining is a highly specialized and dangerous industry which cannot be learned

United Mine Workers President John L. Lewis.

in a day. Few people want to mine coal and fewer still know how. The fact is that the only people who can mine coal or who will mine it are the miners who are accustomed to the hard, dirty, toilsome job.

These are the hard facts of life which America has to face. There remains the important question: What kind of man is this John L. Lewis who in this country holds the power, if not the glory?

"Ruthless, brutal, dictatorial, dangerous"—"a friend of the poor"—"a fighter for the oppressed"—"a keeper of his word"—"a great actor"—"a charlatan"—"shrewd, power hungry"—"politically ambitious, politically powerful"—"a defender of free enterprise"—"an able negotiator."

These are but a few of the more respectable adjectives, phrases, and epithets which have been applied to Lewis over the years.

As Solid Fuels Administrator, I spent nearly four years dealing with him, and my estimate of the man differs sharply in some respects from the ones generally held about him.

Take, for instance, the conclusion of most Washington observers—that Lewis is one of the nation's most able negotiators. This may be, but the federal government in its negotiations with Lewis during the war was so desperate for coal that it was in the position of the man with a rope around his neck trying to negotiate with the hangman. Ordinarily, in such cases, if the man who is about to be hanged escapes with his life, he and not the hangman is considered to be the able negotiator.

This was approximately my view when, as Solid Fuels Administrator, I was trying to get enough coal produced to fuel the nation's war machine in its backbreaking task of supplying not only this country but the rest of the United Nations with guns, planes, tanks, and ships. I expressed my views at a meeting of the War Production Board during one of the hectic wartime negotiations with Lewis when I was asked whether I proposed to make an agreement with him. My answer was: "Gentlemen, I would lie down with the devil himself if by so doing we could produce enough coal to win the war." The other members of the War Production Board regarded this as the only possible attitude.

Most of the mine owners who negotiate with Lewis are in a much less favorable position

than the government was during the war. They are in no position to invoke whatever patriotisms he or the mine workers may possess. Hence, to say that Lewis is an able negotiator is only to affirm that the mine owners recognize the inevitable.

A Great Orator

With those who call Lewis a great actor, I would agree. In fact, it is as an actor that Lewis commands my greatest respect. In talking "man to man" in an office, Lewis is as frank and as free of theatricals as any upstanding business man or lawyer. But when he leads the "good men and true" of his policy committee to his side of a conference table, he is as much a tragedian as ever were Sir Henry Irving and Richard Mansfield. And biding his time, Lewis waits for what he regards as a good cue for him to set his thunder to rolling. Then, in a browbeating attitude, he will remind the operators of at least some of the crimes that, according to his view, they have committed.

Lewis can utter the word "hungry" with a sob in his voice that instinctively causes one to tug at his belt and reach for his handkerchief. He seldom fails to try to wring sympathy for the "hungry bellies" of the miners. Curiously enough, during these proceedings, he never expresses concern that the families of the miners may be hungry too, and might benefit from better living conditions and educational opportunities.

When the tears begin to appear in John L. Lewis' voice, the faces of the operators across the table take on a Do-we-have-to-listen-to-this-sort-of-thing-again? expression. But Lewis' supporting cast does not forget its role, each man

A hard-bargaining Lewis presents UMW demands to Wage and Labor Board, 1945.

perhaps having in mind the next salary check that, by the grace of John L. Lewis, will be drawn against the treasury of the United Mine Workers of America. Thomas Kennedy, representing the anthracite area of Pennsylvania and at one time lieutenant governor of that state, looks serious and as unself-conscious as possible. Tears begin to gather in the eyes of Major Percy Tetlow, Lewis' economic adviser. The glowering countenance of John O'Leary somehow gives the impression that he himself practices daily before his mirror in order to excel in unrelieved gloom the expression of John L. Lewis himself. The facial expressions of others in Lewis' entourage vary, but none is forgetful that if a wandering glance from the great man should detect even a fleeting expression of annoyance or amusement, except in imitation of Lewis, the culprit might have to go back to wielding a pick and shovel underground.

Operators See Sham

Among the operators are one or two, Charles O'Neil and O. L. Alexander—both men for whom Lewis is said to have a somewhat high personal regard—upon whom he customarily turns with particular virulence. The operators recognize that Mr. Lewis is merely putting on an act for the benefit of his assembled policy committee, "the boys" who, as he well knows, will go back to their respective districts and tell about John L.'s stellar performance.

Furthermore, the operators have long memories and a fair degree of intelligence, so that they are aware that there is a considerable degree of sham in Mr. Lewis' wailing for the "hungry bellies" of the miners. They remember that back in the '20s Mr. Lewis, as president of the United Mine Workers, Herbert Hoover, then Secretary of Commerce, and some of the big mine operators agreed to a $7.50-a-day scale for miners, deciding that the trouble with the coal industry was that it had too many mines and too many miners. The $7.50-a-day scale agreed upon would have pushed many of the high-cost mines out of business, thus reducing the number of mines, and hence the number of miners. All told, had the plan worked, some 200,000 miners and their families would have been forced out of the coal industry. Presumably they would have found work in other fields of industrial activity, if they had not starved to death first.

Ruthless, Power-Hungry

Such cold, calculating, and ruthless decisions are part and parcel of Lewis' equipment. This incident would seem to belie his pretensions to being "the miners' best friend." In fact, the longer his record is studied, the more it becomes apparent that he is not concerned primarily with all of the coal miners or their families. He has, for instance, for years harassed the Progressive Miners of America, a group in Illinois which is independent of the United Mine Workers. As late as two years ago the Attorney General of the United States spent some time investigating reports that the mine workers union, or its affiliates, had subsidized a mine operator in Illinois so that he could afford to break a strike of members of the Progressive Miners. Further, it is apparent that Lewis has no use for even all of the miners in the mine workers' union. Ray Edmundson spent most of his life as a coal miner, yet when he attempted two years ago to run against Lewis for president of the union, he was not only denied a place on the ballot, he was virtually run out of the union. He is now selling insurance. The fact is that Mr. Lewis is not so much concerned about miners as he is about Lewis. He is after power, the more power the better.

Some have questioned the sincerity of his advocacy of "free enterprise." I do not. He is a firm believer in the dominance of the strongest. And he knows well that the mine workers' union, with its monopoly over the production of coal, is the most powerful economic group in the country.

"Keeps His Word"?

"Lewis always keeps his word" is another stock phrase always used to describe the mine workers' chieftain, and Mr. Lewis himself is not averse to vaunting this alleged fact.

An experience of mine as Solid Fuels Administrator throws some light on this claim. In the fall of 1944, when this country badly needed coal, strike after strike plagued the coal regions, although Lewis in signing the contract had stipulated that there would be no strikes if the operators lived up to their agreements. Mr.

Lewis failed to cite any operator as refusing to live up to the agreement, nevertheless the strikes continued. Lewis' excuse this time was that the strikes were no strikes of *mine workers*, but merely strikes of members of the supervisory force.

Of course a mine could not be operated without its foremen. It would have been just as effective from Mr. Lewis' point of view, but more honest, if he had frankly closed down the mine. Since the mine foremen had just been initiated into District No. 50 of the mine workers' union —Lewis' union—this was an obvious subterfuge.

I came to suspect that there were occasions when he would not order the miners out in open violation of his agreement, but they would go out just the same when an interruption of work by a strange coincidence would seem to serve the purpose of the dictator. The fact is that I found Lewis to be a keeper of the letter and not of the spirit of the agreements that he made.

The famous Lewis scowl.

In labor-union politics he is unpredictable, except that he may be depended upon to be peripatetic. He left the A. F. of L. to lead in organizing the C.I.O. Then he sulked his way out of the C.I.O. and set up bachelor quarters for himself and his men. Recently the A. F. of L. rolled out the red carpet for him and, like a Roman conqueror returning from the provinces, he resumed power and authority in that organization, apparently with the idea of undoing the C.I.O. altogether if he can. In due course many expect him to take over the A. F. of L. as his own, in which event he might deign to change its name to "American Federation of Lewis."

The terms "politically ambitious" and "politically powerful," generally linked together, are frequent estimates heard about John L. Lewis. I subscribe to the first; I must qualify the second.

For some time it has been suspected that he would not be averse to becoming Vice-President. Probably he would not demur if Presidential lightning should strike him. His claim to political consideration lies in the size and deliverability of the vote of the United Mine Workers of America. This vote is not only potent but in many instances decisive in the coal-mining areas of such states as Pennsylvania, West Virginia, and Illinois. A man of lesser ambition or of a more just appraisal of his own qualities might be content to influence elections for congressmen, senators, or governors. But there is no horizon to John L. Lewis' estimation of the political availability of John L. Lewis.

His political power is, however, much less than his political ambitions. Formerly he was a stanch Republican. When the New Deal swept into power, he caught the comet by the tail. He was perfectly willing to tell President Roosevelt how to decide grave national and international policy, and when he came to feel that the President was so errant as to think that he could get along without him, Mr. Lewis made up his mind to show just what a potent political hand he held.

When Wendell L. Willkie was a Republican candidate for President in 1940, Mr. Lewis made his plans carefully, expecting that the election would be close and that the votes of the mine workers could be decisive. At what he considered to be the proper time, he took to the air and roared against Roosevelt.

The election results showed that if the mine

workers listened to John L. Lewis, they did not heed him. So overwhelmingly as to be almost unanimous, they voted for Roosevelt, the man to whom they felt they owed thanks for the improvement in their economic status, even if John L. Lewis felt differently. The whole country indulged in a belly laugh at the expense of the circumferential Mr. Lewis—the man who could not gather in the chips when his hand was called.

Disdains Public Opinion

The 1940 election taught Mr. Lewis that discretion is the better part of valor, and during the 1944 campaign he said never a word to indicate how he was going to vote or indeed whether he proposed to vote at all. But he did send his trained seals who drew salaries from the United Mine Workers' treasury (thanks to him) into the coal-mining districts of the country to pass the word that the great man wanted them this time to vote for Dewey. Again the result was the same. Those areas of the country where the mine workers' vote was thickest came through for Franklin D. Roosevelt as usual.

Now that John L. Lewis has been once again graciously received in the White House, one may speculate as to his intentions with respect to 1948. If I were President Truman I would remember the old adage "Soft words butter no parsnips."

As to the charge that Lewis is contemptuous of public opinion, I would agree. This is particularly true when he is operating in his own field—coal. His most amazing display of disdain for public opinion came during the war, when, while the nation was struggling for its very existence, he took his miners out, not once but three times. Such was his power that he could afford to shrug off the criticism of the coal strikers by our soldiers overseas who wrote in the Stars and Stripes: "And so, John L. Lewis, we say to you, damn your coal-black soul."

This, then, is a rough sketch of one whom many regard as the most powerful man in America. On the record, he is arrogant, dictatorial, ruthless, and brutal, a loose keeper of promises, a first-rate though slightly hammy actor, with a consuming desire for political power to match his economic power. He is a man who, by circumstance and temperament, is one of the most dangerous people on the American scene today. To what degree these potentialities for danger become realities depends upon the government of these United States and, in the final analysis, upon the people.

Lewis, as National CIO chairman, opens campaign to organize textile workers, 1937.

Here We Go Buying Votes Again!

by Harold L. Ickes

Secretary of the Interior Harold L. Ickes never hesitated to say what he thought, and in 1946 he had some definite opinions on campaign expenditures.

The United States has always been secretive about the use of money in politics. Secrecy is a natural component of shame. Both parties have spent money lavishly and have been both corrupt and corrupting. The campaign dollar is a changeable dollar. At times it is as sticky as mucilage, and on other occasions it is as hard to hold onto as an energetic eel.

The party machines, generally speaking, have been willing to go on the theory of "live and let live," although it is an accepted part of campaign technique to emit loud cries of pretended virtue when the opposing party seems to be getting more cash for its candidates, who are probably just as undesirable as the ones on the more restricted diet.

No one would deny that there should be a reasonable amount of money available for legitimate expenditures in an election upon which may depend political and social trends of the country for years to come. It stands to reason that voters cannot be given facts and arguments unless there is money for literature and postage, for the hiring of halls and the financing of speakers, for the radio, and even for the humble dodger that frequently seems to serve only to litter up our streets at the cost of the taxpayers.

But it is to be deplored that the total raised for campaign purposes is beyond all reason and that it is becoming worse.

Between now and November, 1948, our federal laws apparently will permit the expenditure of some $9,000,000 to promote the elections of Congressmen and a President. Actually, during the next two years it is likely that some $50,000,000—enough money to build homes for a brigade of war veterans—will be spent for these purposes. Much of this will be misspent and the complete total will never be known.

One does not have to be too cynical in order to believe that our federal election laws are being evaded. They are, with all of the verve and abandon that made the purveying of bathtub gin not only a profitable business venture but a sporting event during the days of the "noble experiment." Our approach to this question of campaign expenditures is more experimental than it is noble.

Ceiling on Spending?

The law provides that no political committee may spend more than $3,000,000 in promoting the election of a Presidential candidate. The passage of this law by the Congress was hailed —perhaps "touted" would be the better word —as putting a ceiling on the expenditures of the Democratic and Republican National Committees. It has, but not on the number of committees.

Not counting the regular national, state, and local committees of the major and minor parties, there were in 1944 nearly 200 such committees collecting and spending money. Three dozen of these independent committees each spent sums ranging from $20,000 to nearly a million dollars in promoting the election of one candidate or another.

No senatorial candidate, under the law, may spend more than $25,000 in fishing for his election, nor may representatives generally spend more than $5,000. But this does not prevent others from paying out money in behalf of candidates to their liking. It is incredible how many philanthropists and well-wishers can be found to produce money for a candidate. Thus, while a candidate for the Senate may legally spend $24,999.99, committees of one kind or another supporting him may, and frequently do, spend several times this amount. The same thing is true of Candidates for the House of Representatives.

In 1944, in all but one of the thirty-three states electing senators, the average expenditures for each candidate were more than the $10,000 that is the yearly salary of a senator. In more than half of the states the total expenditures on behalf of candidates for the Senate were more than $25,000, so far as surface indications showed.

From the beginning, the federal law has attempted to insist upon publicity for campaign contributions and expenditures on the theory that if the people knew who was contributing to a campaign, and how much, they would have a better basis for judging the candidates. But as the law stands, it is almost impossible even to come within hailing distance of achieving this objective.

No Central Reporting

There is no central reporting place, nor is there any uniform system of reporting, so that it is impossible for anyone to ascertain at any given time how much is being or has been spent. Expenses incident to senatorial campaigns are reported to the secretary of the Senate. Similar outlays for representatives are reported to the clerk of the House.

Furthermore, not all of the money spent to promote the election of representatives, senators, or the President is by committees which must by law report. County and city and state committees, which do not have to report expenditures to the federal government, distribute huge sums of money in the aggregate for the election of local and state candidates. Such campaigns are deliberately timed with those in state and in nation in an effort to add to the straight party vote, thus benefiting all candidates up and down the line.

As the law stands, it is almost impossible to acquaint the public, before an election, with the amounts being spent by the various candidates. It is only after the election is over that the voters learn in part the extent to which money was used to influence the electorate. And then it is too late to do any good.

Corporations, banks, and labor unions are forbidden by law to contribute to the campaign funds of any candidate for representative, senator, or President. Ever since the enactment of the Federal Corrupt Practices Act in 1925, corporations generally have taken refuge in these provisions, although as individuals the officers of many corporations have made large contributions as well as "their sisters, their cousins and their aunts." In 1943, as the result of the activity of the Political Action Committee of the C.I.O., the act was amended to forbid contributions by labor unions.

Expenditures For Candidates

Testifying before a Senate Investigating Committee, the P.A.C. has expressed the view that the law forbids *contributions to the campaign funds of a candidate*, but that it does not forbid *expenditures on behalf of a candidate*.

Thus the position of the P.A.C. is that it could not write out a check to the Democratic National Committee to be spent in behalf of the party's candidate, but that *it* could spend as much money as *it* liked in urging the people to vote for the candidates. When pressed by the Senate Investigating Committee, counsel for the P.A.C. said that he thought the same rule would apply to corporations. In his opinion, corporations were forbidden to contribute to the campaign funds of a candidate, but the law did not prohibit them from spending their money to campaign for candidates.

Lavish fund-raising dinners: one way to "buy votes."

If this interpretation of the law prevails, it is obvious that in the 1948 election corporations as well as labor unions may take advantage of it. Yet it is difficult to see how this interpretation can be challenged, for to deny the right of a person or an organization to spend money in behalf of a candidate would be in effect to deny the freedom of speech guaranteed by the First Amendment of the Constitution.

Such an interpretation, however, raises obvious practical difficulties. Who, for instance, shall determine whether a corporation or a labor union should spend money to help elect a Republican, a Democratic, or a Socialist candidate for President?

It may be that the labor unions will live to regret the position taken by the P.A.C. Long ago corporations learned to be grateful for the Federal Corrupt Practices Act, because it gave them an excuse to keep the swarm of political pressure boys from "blackmailing" contributions out of them. Now that the P.A.C. has forced open the door again, it may be that politicians will find opportunities to demand, under a threat of political reprisals, that both corporations and labor unions spend their money to promote the candidacy of this candidate or that, although technically not contributing directly to a candidate or his committee.

Getting Around Law

A further provision of the law is supposed to limit the contribution of any one person to not more than $5,000 in any campaign! This has been evaded easily and persistently by those who are in a position to give large sums. Moreover, there is nothing to prevent a rich individual or family contributing to state or county committees *between* campaigns when there are no candidates running.

Nor are the wealthy families the only ones that are notable in this respect. The $500,000 contribution to the Democratic Party by John L. Lewis out of the United Mine Workers' treasury in the 1936 Presidential campaign was of the same pattern. In this connection it is not without significance that people who are looking for a favor that can come only through the success of a particular candidate or party are not unlikely to be moved to generosity in the direction of the party treasury.

Another great flaw in these laws is that they do not touch or profess to reach the practices which are in vogue in party primaries and conventions. This is a grave oversight because in many states—for instance, the Southern states —the man who captures the primary is assured of election. Or a candidate may win the nomination of both parties, as happened recently in the case of Governor Warren of California. In such instances the cost of getting elected is confined to the primary fight.

Arkansas in the 1944 senatorial campaign provides a good illustration. There the four major Democratic candidates reported that they expended in the primary a total of more than $300,000, the salary of a senator for thirty years. The primary campaign expenses for the victor, Senator Fulbright, were $74,000, while he listed his election campaign expenses at $35.07.

The Corrupt Practices Act, and the Hatch Act which implements it to some extent, were copied in part from the British Corrupt Practices Act. British experience has indicated that the best results in the enforcement of the act were achieved by placing the responsibility for the collection and expenditures of funds upon a single legally authorized political committee. The wording of the Federal Corrupt Practices Act would lead one to believe that this was the hope of its framers. Actually this hope died stillborn.

More Committees

The limitations on expenditures in the Hatch Act have resulted in the proliferation of political committees and the compounding of expenses. In 1944, while both the Democratic and Republican National Committees spent less than the $3,000,000 permitted by law, the total recorded expenditures, through the device of setting up various committees, totaled more than $20,000,000. Many of these committees are closely allied to the national committees, but others work independently.

One of the unfortunate results of this system is that it diminishes the responsibility and authority of the party and permits the formation of irresponsible organizations.

In the aggregate, the sums which are expended to elect the federal officials of the United States are tremendous, even though this is a big country. In the last three decades the number of voters in this country has increased enormously. In 1916, less than 20,000,000 voters went to the polls. In practically every congressional district in the country the number of voters has doubled during the last thirty years. Modern inventions such as sound trucks and radio have added to the cost of a campaign.

Yet, taking all factors into consideration, large sums are put to uses that are not legitimate and do not conduce to the sound political health of the country. There have been closely contested elections, especially in the big cities, where a whole army of "workers" are hired on election day at prices that used to be five dollars a head, but now run to many times that modest amount. This constitutes nothing short of open vote buying.

Acts Need Revision

Obviously, in the face of the tremendous changes in the American political scene and the American way of life and in the light of widespread evasion of the law, our Federal Corrupt Practices Act and the Hatch Act need a major revision if they are to catch up with reality. Such a revision is long overdue. An overhauling has been recommended by every senatorial and House investigation since 1936.

My own belief is that instead of trying to put additional props under a wobbling system, the federal government should finance the campaigns of candidates for federal offices out of the public treasury. This system, if adopted in the nation, would necessarily in course of time

Excessive campaign spending: a continuing American dilemma.

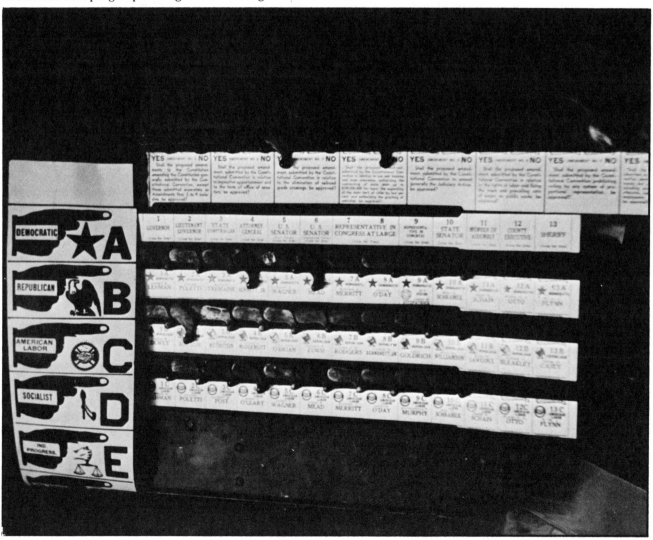

97

be followed in the states.

This is not a revolutionary suggestion. I make no claim to originality in bringing it up. Many years ago the State of Oregon made a start in this direction.

If the theory is correct that in the end the people pay in any event through special privileges and the grant of improper benefits, such as leniency in prosecuting antitrust suits, it would be more straightforward if the nation should frankly adopt the policy of paying legitimate campaign expenses up to a certain point, beyond which no expenses would be permitted.

Temporary But Immediate

In the end it would cost us much less. We have to have elections. Our system of government calls for them, and we ought to pay our own way without being subsidized by those who seek favors or an undue influence in determining national policies. We would then be much more certain to have a free man in the White House and free men in the two houses of Congress.

If, however, we have not yet reached that stage of political maturity that can be expected to look squarely at the facts and act upon them as intelligent men and women, then, as temporary measures, I suggest that there are revisions of our present laws that are immediately needed:

1. Since a limitation on permissible expenditures by national committees has been so crassly set at naught by the organization of other committees, it should be a requirement of the law that there should be only one bona fide national committee for each bona fide party and that no contributions, direct or indirect, including family hope chests, be made except to such a committee.

2. The extension of the laws covering campaign expenses to primaries and conventions.

3. The nullifying of anonymous contributors. On a number of occasions in the past various political committees have tried to hide some of their donors by listing their contributions as "anonymous." In one instance a committee reported that two $1,000 bills were tossed into its office through an open window. I suggest that all such manna-from-heaven contributions be turned over to the government.

4. A central agency to which all political collections and expenditures must be reported is necessary for the strengthening of the publicity features of the law. This agency might well be one of the executive departments and it should be authorized to give out the fullest information. To expedite its work, all reports should be required to be made in a uniform manner.

5. To insure the fullest publicity, duplicates of all reports filed with the central agency should be filed with the clerk of the local U.S. District Court in which the committee operates. In this way, local newspapers and radio stations would have ready access to the material.

6. The end of limits on individual contributions. It seems to me that wealthy contributors in no event would give more than they give now.

Radio, TV Time

So far, the proposals that I have made would seem to favor the rich. As a matter of fact, they would merely legalize practices which are already in existence. The well-to-do might even contribute less than they do now if the publicity proposals were strictly enforced. In any event, it would improve morale all around. One would prefer to be honest and straightforward if possible.

These suggestions do not solve the problem of the poor man who wants to run for office and who deserves a chance at that office if our democracy is to work. To give the man without money a chance and to overcome the decided differential that the candidate who has access to large sums of money now has, my own belief is that all candidates, regardless of how much money they have, ought to be given a certain number of hours on the radio in any campaign. Radio stations could hardly object to this, since they are now required by law to devote a good many hours each week to programs "in the public interest."

With television almost upon us, it is important that every candidate be given a chance to appear on television programs. I am not suggesting here that any limits be placed on the amount of time that a candidate may buy, but only that all candidates should have a reasonable opportunity for a minimum amount of time.

Muscling In on Labor

by Victor Riesel and Will Chasan

In 1946, Victor Riesel, top labor columnist, and Will Chasan exposed racketeer infiltration of the labor unions.

It would have been an unusual picket line. Some highly incensed delegates to the recent annual convention of the New York State Federation of Labor convention in Rochester were planning to demonstrate against a high-handed political deal by some of their leaders. But the demonstration never came off.

One of the federation's moguls, hearing that he was to be picketed and unwilling to be subjected to his own brand of pressure, had quietly placed a phone call to New York City. Several hours before the picketing was to begin, a grimly efficient-looking man, who would have fitted neatly into the cast of a gangster movie, flew into Rochester. He sought out the leader of the A.F.L. insurgents. "You going to picket?" he asked.

"Yes," said the insurgent.

"O.K., then," came the calm, professional reply. "Where would you like to be dumped, in the river or the lake?"

The insurgent, having no taste for martyrdom, promptly decided not to picket. But he asked his menacing interrogator, well known in the underworld, "What are you doing in this area? I didn't think you operated around here."

The answer he got was, "We operate from here to California."

Unfortunately, the man was not exaggerating. Murder, Inc., the Capone gang, and the other national crime syndicates are gone. But their remnants, linked together under the lieutenants of the late and unmourned mobsters who made newspaper headlines, are still in business. What is more, from coast to coast they are now becoming more aggressive. Knowing the black market can't last forever as a source of easy revenue, and with other war-

Labor columnist Victor Riesel, known for exposing union corruption.

time rackets drying up, they are methodically reaching out for new ones. In this new surge of mobster imperialism, unions are not being overlooked.

Until a few months ago, reports of mobsters moving in on labor were largely night-club and newspaper-city-room gossip. Since then, however, in many of the country's big cities the successors of Lepke and Capone, some of them tougher and greedier than the men they succeeded, have begun to maneuver for control of a number of wealthy and powerful unions. Simultaneously, many of the old labor racketeers, sensing a new era of low morality and high profits, have begun to reassert themselves.

99

For example, "Umbrella" Mike Boyle, a convicted crook whom a Chicago Court of Appeals once characterized as a "blackmailer, highwayman, betrayer of labor, and leech on commerce," has again become a power in the big International Brotherhood of Electrical Workers (A.F.L.)—a union able to turn off the current in a large section of American industry.

Last summer, at the I.B.E.W. convention in San Francisco, Umbrella Mike led a bloc of delegates in ousting the union's international president and in electing to the presidency Dan Tracy, until recently Assistant Secretary of Labor. This makes Boyle a power in the I.B.E.W., regardless of Tracy's honesty.

In St. Louis, John "Big" Nick, now on parole from Leavenworth and who before the war ran with the Capone syndicate, has been trying to take over the International Alliance of Theatrical Stage Employees, once the private domain of the master extortionist Willie Bioff. Big Nick was jailed in 1940, after having been convicted of violating the federal Anti-Racketeering Act on eleven counts. He was then a business agent of the St. Louis Motion Picture Operators Union, and controlled the stagehands there, too. After his release from Leavenworth, he and his goons tried to take over the affluent unions of stagehands and motion-picture operators in St. Louis by strong-arm tactics. There were bloody brawls and the police had to be called in to protect the members at their own meetings. Nevertheless, Nick's men continued to discourage attendance at union sessions, and a few months ago, at a meeting attended by less than 100 persons, Nick came within one vote of electing a henchman to the union presidency.

He was stopped only when Richard T. Walsh, the I.A.T.S.E. president who cleaned house after Bioff went to jail, stepped in and seized the St. Louis locals. Now the parole board is investigating Nick.

Slimy Hymie

In New York, a man named Palatnik, and known to some persons as "Slimy Hymie," is reported to have taken over a section of the International Jewelry Workers, an affiliate of the American Federation of Labor. He is one of several persons who have recently turned up in the jewelry industry with organizing jurisdictions.

New Yorkers first heard of Palatnik in January, 1945, when officials of the Bulova Watch Co. testified before a National Labor Relations Board hearing that they had been threatened with "plenty of trouble" unless they paid a jewelry workers local $15,000. One of those who testified was Arde Bulova, chairman of the Bulova board, who revealed he had been promised that a "Joey Rao's mob" would protect him against the C.I.O. and independent unions if the company made a deal with the A.F.L. jewelry workers outfit run by Palatnik.

Bulova said that Palatnik had sent an emissary to him to say: "We're not so interested in organizing as in making a piece of money. If we could make a deal with you we'd go somewhere else." And, Bulova said, the emissary added: "I'm Hymie Palatnik's right-hand man. I work with him. . . . You make a deal with us and Joey Rao's mob will take care of you. He's financing Palatnik. He'll take care of all the unions."

Today, a handful of C.I.O. men, organized in a competing union, are fighting Palatnik's efforts to expand in the jewelry field.

Joe Fay A Real Force

It is common knowledge that Joe Fay, a New Jersey building-union official who has been convicted of extorting hundreds of thousands of dollars from construction contractors, is still one of the country's powerful union chiefs. A New Jersey governor once described him, with no great bruising of the truth, as "one of the real forces in American life."

The New Jersey boss is probably best remembered as the man who knocked down David Dubinsky at an A.F.L. convention because the International Ladies Garment Workers Union president introduced an anti-racketeering resolution, thus offending his sensibilities. In addition to his union job, Fay has a trucking and excavating business, and is said to be enormously wealthy. Convicted of extortion last year, his appeal is still pending, and he is still pulling strings in New Jersey-New York labor circles.

The mobsters, who rarely overlook an opportunity, also have been casing America's booming chemical and plastic industries. They see in this industry of hundreds of small busi-

ness units and weak unions a sphere tailor-made for their operations.

Not long ago an Eastern mob sent a "messenger" to the manager of a small plastic workers union. The message was simple. "Look," the tough said, "the boys want you to play ball. If you don't, they're going to be pretty upset." He made it plain to the union manager that any failure to co-operate would probably end in his being murdered.

And during the recent runaway strike in the New York trucking industry, long a mobster stronghold, some of the hoodlums showed their hand. Though the public was unaware of it, one of the demands made by some rank-and-file strike leaders was the junking of a "supplementary clause" in the contract which barred New York teamsters from taking trucks beyond the Hackensack River in New Jersey. This clause was something the New York mobs, operating through sections of the Teamsters Union, had objected to for years because it limited the area over which they could use gangster tactics on New York drivers. Mayor O'Dwyer charged that Communists were prolonging the strike, but the charge could have been leveled with greater accuracy aginst the mobsters.

Anyone reading through the new agreement will see that the clause has been dropped.

Furthermore, all through the so-called "uncontrollable" strike, it was possible for truck owners to obtain drivers and to have their vans "escorted" through the tough, roving picket lines.

"There are three telephone numbers the operators can call for protection," one of the highest Teamsters Brotherhood officials told the writers during the damaging walkout which cut food and newsprint from New Yorkers. The telephone numbers were those of one prominent New Jersey and two Manhattan gang leaders, it was said.

Mob On N.Y. Waterfront

The mobs also are active again along the New York water front. The kickback and loan-shark rackets, on which some of the hoodlum fraternity thrived, were badly dented during the war, but it is said there that organized cargo thefts and extortion are flourishing once more.

Among the influential men on the New York water front is John "Cockeye" Dunn, who has a formidable reputation. He has managed an A.F.L. federal local of platform loaders since 1935. The A.F.L. issued a charter to him for this local, although he had previously served a three-year sentence in Sing Sing for robbery.

He went to jail again in 1942 for coercive action during a wartime strike which kept two British freighters from joining a convoy. But on his release he resumed his position and still holds it. The A.F.L. has not seen fit to act against him, though during his trial in 1942 the head of the New York rackets bureau charged he was the leader of one of four mobs which had turned the New York water front into a "Western outlaw frontier." It is a matter of record that five men have been killed in a war over control of a single I.L.A. local.

Dunn's case is especially interesting because it involves a local holding an A.F.L. federal charter. These charters are issued directly by

Union leader Joseph F. Fay on his way to jail for extortion and conspiracy.

the A.F.L. office in Washington. Anyone who has the necessary connection with the A.F.L. officialdom and is willing to pay per capita tax for a handful of members can get one. The federal locals are not subject to check or investigation by any agency except the national A.F.L. office and its regional directors. The laxity of these agents in all matters except per capita tax collection is notorious. As a result, hoodlums often have been able to use such locals in establishing themselves in the labor business.

A prize example of this is the operations of Ben Pross, currently the executive secretary of the New York branch of the Wine, Liquor, and Distillery Workers Union. Pross, who has served two jail terms for fraud and has been indicted and fined once for black-market liquor sales, has at one time or another been associated with seventeen unions, most of them federal locals. The A.F.L. officials in Washington, who are aware of Pross's record, as they are of Dunn's, have never done anything to discourage his participation. Officially they merely point out that they are much too busy with national and international matters to police thousands of small federal locals throughout the nation.

The hoodlum fraternity gets its money in many different ways. It extorts money from employers whose workers it controls, using the threat to strike as a club. It collects fat sums from employers in return for signing agreements which constitute a "sellout" of the workers. The mobsters also do a huge business in selling non-union employers protection against union organizers.

In most cases employers who hire hoodlums to protect them from unions live to regret it. There is one Eastern manufacturer who had paid a mobster $25,000 a year for the past ten years, and is unable to shake him. When the wartime boom came along, and with it closer government surveillance of rackets, some of the racketeers decided that it was bad economics to take merely "protection" money, and they "bought out" the manufacturers they had been protecting.

Manufacturers and labor officials who, for one reason or another, have been forced into dealings with the mobs say that the mob leaders now are even more onerous than when Lepke and Gurrah ruled the underworld.

These incidents are not isolated. Regrettably, they are part of a pattern emerging in many of our large industries. A veteran labor official who has been watching the gangs' renewed activities since V-J Day told the writers recently, "I don't think we're going to have a repetition of the days when the Capone mobs had more power in the A.F.L. than John Lewis, when they threw bombs, looted union treasuries, and kidnaped union leaders. But there is going to be trouble."

All this may surprise those who believed that the F.B.I. and a few tough district attorneys had squelched all the racketeers. Unfortunately, more racketeers were disposed of in newspaper headlines than in reality, though labor today is cleaner than at any time since the late '20s when the racketeers first fanned out in the labor movement.

The C.I.O. has been free of gangsters because because most of its leaders and organizers —such as young James Carey, national C.I.O. secretary, and Walter Reuther, auto union president—are ardent crusaders who swung into the C.I.O. to get away from old-line union practices. Some of the C.I.O.'s affiliates, however, are beset by a form of political corruption that has cost C.I.O. members hundreds of thousands of dollars. This corruption is centerd in the small but voluble section of the C.I.O. controlled by Communists.

These Communist-dominated unions have spent large sums helping to finance the "peace," "civil liberties," foreign relief, and political front organizations created by the Communist Party in the past decade.

Honest labor officials eye the future with misgiving. They know that a revival of open labor racketeering, no matter how limited its scope, will again blacken labor before the public and create a vicious problem for them.

"It is easy for people to criticize labor for failing to curb racketeers," one prominent union official said, "and some of this criticism is obviously justified. But how can the public expect labor officials to clean up racketeers whom the F.B.I., district attorneys, and police forces have failed to apprehend? How can we succeed where the government, with its vast power, has failed?"

That, for the American public no less than for labor, is going to be the sixty-four-dollar question in the months ahead.

Horse-and-Buggy Diplomacy Is Hurting Us

by James Reston

James B. Reston, Pultizer Prize winning writer for the New York Times, *said in 1947 that the U.S. was playing a new global role with old equipment.*

The United States sent a new team to Moscow this month to negotiate with the Russians on peace treaties for Germany and Austria. This mission is being directed by Secretary of State George C. Marshall. The team we sent to Moscow in December, 1945, was run by James F. Byrnes. Earlier in 1945 the American Secretary of State at the Yalta Conference was Edward R. Stettinius, Jr. And when the first meeting of the Big Three Foreign Ministers was held in the Soviet capital in October, 1943, Cordell Hull was Secretary of State and led our delegation.

A new captain almost every year and plenty of eager new substitutes on the team may be an excellent system for football but it is not necessarily good for diplomatic negotiations involving the peace of the world. The United States is trying to create a just and stable peace. World stability depends in great measure upon the continuity and stability of the policies of the great powers; and our personnel changes have not been conductive to creating a sense of American stability.

As a matter of fact, our policy has remained fairly stable in the period from Cordell Hull to George Marshall. In this era of personal journalism and authoritarian governments, however, the world has come to think of contemporary history in terms of individuals, and the inevitable effect of so many changes is uncertainty, especially when we have changed our team at the United Nations almost as fast as we have changed it at the Department of State. In the first year of the U. N. Security Council, for example, we had four different negotiators: Stettinius, Byrnes, Herschel Johnson, and former Senator Warren R. Austin. This

was the worst case, but in the other agencies of the U. N., the same now-you-see-'em-and-now-you-don't situation existed.

Rapid Turnover

Eugene Meyer, former publisher of the Washington Post, took over the presidency of the World Bank, a U. N. affiliated agency, and gave it up after a few months. Much was made of the fact that we were taking our Ambassador from London, John Winant, in order to have a strong U. S. delegation to the U. N. Economic and Social Council, but Mr. Winant also retired after the first few meetings.

Similarly, Bernard M. Baruch, given almost an autonomous status in directing our A-bomb policy in the U. N. Atomic Energy Commission, resigned while the negotiations were still in a formative stage. Finally, Senator Arthur H. Vandenberg of Michigan and Senator Tom Connally of Texas, who did so much to make the United Nations a reality, say they cannot continue to take time out from their duties on Capitol Hill to participate in future meetings of the Council of Foreign Ministers and the United Nations.

If the fundamentals of American foreign policy were deeply rooted in tradition and history, and if we had a stable and reliable Civil Service to help direct policy from one Secretary of State to another and from one national administration to another, these changes would not seem so important. But this is not the case.

Look at the problem for a moment from the point of view of the world's Foreign Ministers who have come to this country recently. Those who came to the last meeting of the General Assembly in New York found the United States was represented in the main political committee meetings by Senator Connally. Not only did Secretary Byrnes stay away until the very end, when he made one set speech to the

Assembly, but the principal U. S. delegate, Warren Austin, did not negotiate for the United States on the main committees.

As a result, Senator Connally was not only overworked and negotiating at a disadvantage against two Foreign Secretaries, but on at least two occassions his remarks were repudiated by members of the State Department, who explained to the press that the senator did not on these occasions represent the U. S. position accurately.

World Reputation At Stake

The world's Foreign Ministers are constantly confronted with situations in which they must decide whether or not they can rely on a stable American policy, and when American negotiators are ineffective or overwhelmed by other negotiators, their confidence is impaired and our reputation as a world leader is not enhanced.

The experience of the Italian Prime Minister on his recent trip to Washington is perhaps the best illustration of the unsettling effect of our casual personnel policy. Alice de Gasperi came here last Christmas. He was in the same position as most European Foreign Ministers, fighting the left-right battle at home and needing economic aid from the United States. He held a series of solemn conferences with Mr. Byrnes; and then, after he felt that he understood our position, he prepared to leave for home. Just at this point, Mr. Byrnes resigned, and the letters of resignation showed clearly that, without de Gasperi's knowledge, Mr. Byrnes had actually known he was resigning throughout their conversations. De Gasperi got a promise of help, but what he reported to his Cabinet about U. S. negotiating procedures is not known.

Changing Role of U.S.

It is easier to explain why these things happen than to correct them. The explanation lies primarily in the fact that the United States is playing a new role in the world with old equipment—old in years and old in habits. No nation in the world, with the possible exception of the Soviet Union, has been pitchforked into a position of world leadership so quickly as has

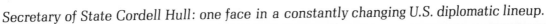

Secretary of State Cordell Hull: one face in a constantly changing U.S. diplomatic lineup.

105

the United States. In spite of all the talk about a bipartisan foreign policy, we have not yet achieved a wholly American policy in all fields.

For nearly a century the United States has been an "observer" of world affairs, and for nearly a hundred years of its independent existence it was a debtor naticn, borrowing money abroad to develop its resources and raising tariff barriers to protect its developing industries.

Now, suddenly, it is neither an observer nor a debtor. It is a leader of world relations and the wealthiest creditor nation in history. The change in the debtor-creditor status has taken place in a generation; the change from observer to leader in less than a decade.

Inevitably, there is always a gap between the acceptance of a new idea by a large electorate and the implementation of that idea into the laws and habits of the country. This lag afflicts not only the people but their executives. Franklin Roosevelt was one of the greatest advocates of the idea that foreign affairs were of vital importance; yet, in selecting a successor to Cordell Hull as Secretary of State, he chose a man who had very little background for the job. Similarly, Mr. Byrnes often spoke of the mission of world peace as the most important in the world; but when a convenient time arrived for him to resign, he got out, though, his health was certainly no worse than Ernest Bevin's or Andrei Vishinsky's, both of whom have carried on.

There is also a relevant hangover of political habits, and this also helps explain the selection of certain U. S. representatives and the rejection of others. For example, no American at the San Francisco Conference was more effective as a negotiator or made a better impression on his world colleagues than Harold Stassen. He was more responsible than any other delegate at that conference for the drafting of the U. N. trusteeship charter, but he was passed over when it came time to select the American delegation to the first United Nations General Assembly meeting in London.

Instead, Frank Walker, former Democratic national chairman, and John G. Townsend, Jr., chairman of the Republican Senatorial Committee, were chosen to supplement the U. S. delegates who had been at San Francisco. Senator Fullbright complained about this at the time and suggested that they had been chosen for political reasons, that President Truman had explained that he wanted to "pass these jobs around."

Why The Instability?

Also for political reasons, the President has kept on the American delegations to the United Nations General Assembly the leading Republican and Democratic members of the House Foreign Affairs Committee and the Senate Foreign Relations Committee.

This had proved to be wise, particularly in the case of Senators Vandenberg and Connally; but the roles assigned to these men, and particularly to Representatives Charles Eaton of New Jersey and Sol Bloom of New York, have not always been so carefully selected. For example, the idea originally was that these representatives of Congress would be *advisers* to the delegation. Instead, they were allowed to do a great deal of the actual *negotiating*, and while Mr. Vandenberg proved himself an adept negotiator, capable of dealing with the best of the foreign delegates, the others did not always represent the United States as well as it could have been represented.

Here again the reason was a hangover from old customs. We had learned to our sorrow, through the experience of Woodrow Wilson, that Congress had to be represented in the negotiation of international agreements. This mistake we corrected, but in doing so we assigned to some of the Congressional representatives tasks that were sometimes beyond their capacities. And the excuse given, perhaps a valid one under the circumstances, was that the executive branch of the government could not afford to antagonize the legislature.

Thus, in some ways, we are not only the prisoners of habit but of the Constitution. In explaining why we have difficulty in attaining a greater degree of continuity at the Department of State, we have merely to consider the number and ages of past secretaries, the salaries paid to top Civil Service officials in Washington, and the vast increase in the staff of the State Department in the last few years.

Since we submit each administration to the test of a general election every four years, this fact alone imposes many changes. For example, in the long period between Thomas

Jefferson and George Marshall, only five Secretaries of State have held the office for as long as eight years. The average is just over three years. And in the last three years we have had four heads of the department. This problem might have been minimized if the Secretary of State, like the British Foreign Secretary, were backed up by a permanent Civil Service that maintained continuity at the policy level. But the United States has never been able to offer sufficient reward, in terms of money or position, to develop such a staff. While a few men of private means like William L. Clayton and Dean Acheson have stayed on in top positions from the Stettinius to the Marshall regimes, they have been the exception rather than the rule.

All these factors help explain *why* there are mistakes, inefficiency, and instability in the conduct of our foreign affairs, but they do not remove the dangers from instability.

Possible Solutions

What can be done about it? The first thing is that the bipartisan approach to foreign problems must be continued and expanded. In the past two years it has dealt mainly with United Nations and Russian policy, and in these fields of policy it has been effective; but it has not as yet touched the other fields of policy—particularly the foreign economic field—and foreign politics and foreign economics can be separated only at our peril.

There is, admittedly, a limit beyond which bipartisan co-operation in the planning and execution of foreign policy cannot go. The President is charged by the Constitution with the conduct of foreign affairs. He must be responsible for it. Moreover, he and the Secretary of State and their aides are the only officials who have all the information necessary to make policy. But wherever policy requires

Secretary of State James F. Byrnes (right) with Soviet Foreign Minister V. M. Molotov at Big Four Conference in Paris, 1946.

the consent or financial support of Congress, bipartisan consultation must be sought, and it has not always been sought by Democrats or offered by Republicans.

Another idea worth exploring is the creation of a General Planning Staff at the State Department and a Diplomatic Academy. When Elihu Root came into the War Department as Secretary at the turn of the century, he reorganized the department, planned the new War College, and instituted the General Staff to work out long-range plans. Many observers in Washington feel that much the same must be done at the Department of State.

Specifically; it has been suggested that there should be a more elaborate training school for State Department and foreign-service officers on the order of West Point and Annapolis. Such an academy, some observers feel, would encourage a much broader element of the nation's youth to enter the diplomatic service and eventually provide the manpower to run our expanding foreign policy.

Meanwhile, it is generally felt in the capital, greater opportunities and higher salaries must be given to younger men at the Department of State and in the foreign service. Two of the most promising of the younger men in the State Department in recent years were Mr. Dickey and Alger Hiss. The former left the department to become president of Dartmouth College, and the latter—in charge of drafting our United Nations policy—took a more lucrative job with the Carnegie Foundation.

There seems to be something approaching a doctrine that the Secretary of State must be a venerable gentleman of the old school. Daniel Webster was sixty-eight when he headed the department for the second time; Henry L. Stimson was sixty-one when he succeeded Frank B. Kellogg in 1929; and Cordell Hull was sixty-one when he took the job and seventy-three when he resigned. Ed Stettinius was one exception; but Mr. Byrnes was sixty-seven when he quit, and General Marshall was sixty-six when he took office.

This question of age is much more important now than it was even a decade ago. Experience, admittedly, is necessary for the job; but the routine of a Secretary of State today entails not only a killing job at home but a wearisome and persistent series of long journeys abroad. In the future we are going to have to think of younger and stronger men of the generation of William Fulbright, Joseph Ball, Harold Stassen, Dean Acheson, and John Dickey for the position.

In short, under our present system, we are not only handicapped by a rapid turn-over of our foreign-policy negotiators at the top, but we are losing many of the best of the younger men in the department. It is a casual and spendthrift system and we can no longer afford it.

The New Truman

by Alden Hatch

In 1947, talk about possible 1948 candidates was already in the air, and Alden Hatch assessed one GOP possibility.

In November, 1946, President Harry S. Truman finally put aside the engulfing cloak of his predecessor and stepped out briskly in his own well-cut business suit. The appreciation of the people is evidenced by his rise in the Gallup polls from a low of 32 per cent in October, 1946, to 60 per cent in April, 1947.

Not that the President pays any heed to polls—or labels—as far as his actions are concerned. Once I reminded him that Franklin Roosevelt had said of himself that he was "a little left of center," and asked, "Where do you consider that you stand?" The President replied that he did not bother about right or left, but only about what was right for the people—not of America alone, but of all the world. He added that, whatever the columnists might say, he did not act from political motives. That, I am certain, is the literal truth.

This opinion is backed by a notable authority. General Eisenhower said of his commander in chief:

"Of this I am sure—the President has put personal ambition out of his heart."

I talked with the President a few months after Potsdam. Then he was a sad and lonely man. Potsdam was perhaps the worst ordeal ever faced by an American President. Thrown into that great arena without adequate knowledge of the secret negotiations of the previous administration, following in the footsteps of the towering figure of Franklin Roosevelt, the President clung to his friend Jimmy Byrnes, who, after all, had been at Yalta. But Byrnes himself was uncertain and bewildered, attempting to shape a policy from his memory of what Roosevelt had said he would do; trying to fathom how the master of improvisation would have acted. An impossible task!

The President is very different now. He is a calm and forceful man, bending all his expanding knowledge and ability to a high endeavor. Before our recent meeting I watched him at a press conference. He was clearly enjoying himself. He stood behind his desk on the balls of his feet, like a boxer. Alert and smiling, he swung sharply to right or left to answer the questions fired at him, or to parry them expertly. There was no doubt of his confident authority.

At Home In Washington

The Trumans are now as much at home in the White House as they ever were in Independence, Missouri. The President still rises at 5.30 A.M., and at seven goes for a brisk walk with a Secret Service man, greeting startled early risers with a wave and a smile. He has not changed his basic tastes: he takes his customary two drinks of bourbon a day and likes best to spend his leisure time playing the piano or reading history or military memoirs—he is a leading authority on the strategy of the Civil War.

The new Harry Truman, out of F.D.R.'s shadow.

The President loves a good game of poker and plays his cards high, wide, and handsome. But as he settles down to the unremitting strain of his work, these pleasant evenings are less and less frequent.

Of all the perquisites of the Presidency, the one Truman gets the most fun out of is the Sacred Cow. He hates trains and is sick on ships, but he loves to fly. He is a hell-for-leather type of flyer, and on Christmas Day, 1945, he flew out to see his mother in Missouri through snow and sleet that grounded commercial planes. Mrs. Truman and Mary Margaret don't like flying. However, the President has many friends who do. He loads the Sacred Cow up with as many of them as she will hold—preferably poker players—and sets off, with his pilot, Lieutenant Colonel Henry T. Meyers, at the controls.

Mrs. Truman is a completely charming hostess whose unaffected hospitality makes the atmosphere of the White House one of gracious simplicity. Mary Margaret, who is more interested in a musical career than in the ephemeral glitter of being the President's daughter, lives mostly in New York, but when she is home the rugs come up in the Blue Room and the young people of Washington arrive to dance the samba and eat a buffet supper.

The recent change in Harry Truman has been variously ascribed to new advisers, a difference of the political climate, or a change in his nature. The fact is that it is not change, but growth.

This does not imply that the President has not some good advisers. By trial and error he has acquired an excellent little Brain Trust. John R. Steelman, John W. Snyder, Charles G. Ross, Major General Harry H. Vaughan, Clark Clifford, and Matthew J. Connelly counsel him on domestic policy; while on foreign and military matters he draws upon the wisdom of Admiral William D. Leahy, Secretary of State Marshall, whom the whole nation trusts and even the Russians respect, and General Eisenhower, whose broad knowledge of the world situation is illumined by an extraordinary clarity of thought and a selfless passion for liberty. Nevertheless, it is the President himself who determines the policy of the government.

There are four factors in the President's character that are fundamentals of the man.

One is his integrity—this is absolute. A second is his idealism, which is tempered by the Missourian's characteristic caution. The third is his kindliness, which sometimes overrides his judgment. The last is his ability to grow.

Very American Boyhood

Harry Truman's life story is an account of the growth of a man. It is not a steady progression but a series of great advances, followed by apparently static periods. The story is divided neatly into chapters, each sharply defined.

First there is his boyhood in Missouri, a very American, Tom Sawyerish chapter of farms and small neat towns like Independence. Harry's father, John Truman, raised and traded in livestock. There were chores for a boy to do and, as he grew older, jobs to earn a little much-needed cash.

Though Harry Truman was a tough and wiry boy, he was not fond of sport—he got plenty of exercise through plain hard work. He loved best to read. In western Missouri, education was a luxury; a book was still a precious thing.

Harry also had a surprisingly deep love of music, and his mother pinched pennies to give him piano lessons. That was really a luxury.

He graduated from high school in 1901, at the age of 17—it was the end of his formal education. There was no money for college. The family had a little influence and got the boy appointed to West Point. Harry might have known it was no use—with those weak eyes of his. He failed the physical examination.

That was the end of Chapter One, of boyhood. Then came an interim when he worked first as clerk and then as bookkeeper in various Kansas City banks. Harry's banking career closed when his uncle Harrison Young decided to retire and offered his prosperous Grandview farm to John Truman and his sons, Harry and Vivian. Harry was twenty-five. For the next ten years he was almost completely happy; the farm prospered and for the first time the Trumans had a real sense of security.

It ended abruptly on April 6, 1917, when the United States entered the war against Germany. Harry Truman had been a member of the Missouri National Guard since 1905—he firmly believes that it is every citizen's duty to

Truman sworn in as 32nd President on April 12, 1945, following Roosevelt's death.

be prepared to fight for his country. He was commissioned as a first lieutenant of artillery.

There followed one of Truman's periods of rapid growth. He learned fast, not only how to shoot guns, but how to lead men. On September 6, 1918, Captain Harry Truman was commanding Battery D, 129th Field Artillery in the Vosges Mountains of France. We have a glimpse of him standing in a downpour behind his four 75s, giving the order to fire. Almost instantly the reply from a battery of German howitzers turns the clearing into pandemonium. Horses are kicking and screaming, men are groping through the smoke and mud. Hysteria sweeps the men. They stampede for safety; then halt, as a rapid fire of oaths jars them back to sanity. Captain Truman is standing in the middle of his battery. His first printable words are, "Come back and help me hitch up the teams and get these guns out of here!"

They got the guns out, and fought them through St. Mihiel and the Argonne down to the village of Hermaville, where they stopped at 10.45 A.M., November 11, 1918.

Harry Truman stayed in the service for a while after the war, rising to the rank of major. Then, with an army pal named Eddie Jacobson, he started the famous haberdashery shop in Kansas City. It failed in the flash depression of 1921.

So Harry was more than broke—he owed a large sum of money. And he had taken a wife. Bess Wallace had gone to school with Harry Truman in Independence. Through nearly twenty years, whether he lived in Kansas City or Grandview, he always managed to get back

Capt. Harry Truman on horseback
in France during World War I.

Truman, who co-owned a Kansas City men's shop from 1919 to 1922, had more success with
politics than haberdashery.

113

to Independence to see her. They were married on June 28, 1919, and moved into the big white house that has been their home ever since.

Enter Boss Pendergast

After the failure of the shop, help came from an unexpected direction. Jim Pendergast, a nephew of Boss Tom Pendergast of Kansas City, had served for a while under Captain Truman and, like all his men, had grown to love him. Now Jim came to him and suggested that Uncle Tom would like Harry to run for county judge of the Eastern District of Jackson County. This was not a legal position, but a managerial one. Judges were chosen for integrity, not for legal ability.

Harry Truman had no illusions about Uncle Tom, but his case was desperate. Not so desperate, however, as to keep him from going to see the Boss and saying, "I want to make it clear that if I should get elected, I won't be mixed up in any monkey business."

The Boss grinned and promised, "No monkey business."

Truman won the election, and worked hard at his new job. Then, in the Democratic rout of 1924, he was defeated. He held odd jobs for two years, and in 1926 Pendergast nominated him for presiding judge of the County Court. He was elected by 16,000 votes.

For the next eight years Truman served Jackson County in that capacity, and even his enemies agree he served it well. There was the matter of the $11,000,000 bond issue for badly needed roads and public buildings. The people were loath to vote for it, because they argued from experience that a large amount of the money would find its way into Boss Pendergast's pockets. Truman said to Pendergast, "I'm going to tell the taxpayers just what I am going to do with the money, and then I will keep my word."

Boss Tom said, "If you can get them to vote for it, you can do as you please."

Truman publicly promised the voters that every contract would be let to the lowest bidder. They evidently believed him, for they voted the bond issue. Then the contractors put on the squeeze. They got nowhere with Truman, so they went to Pendergast.

Truman got a telephone call from the Boss to come over to see him. He found the little office crowded with beefy men who were arguing loudly. Pendergast held up a large hand

Truman (second row, third from right) with fellow officers in France.

114

to quiet them. "Harry," he said, "I want you to explain about our agreement on the bond issue."

"You promised that there were to be no favors or politics in spending the money," Truman said flatly.

The Boss shrugged his huge shoulders. "You see, gentlemen," he said. "I promised."

Crooked though he was, Pendergast had the curious honor of the old-fashioned politician —he was loyal to his friends and he always kept his word. Years later, when the Boss died, a poverty-stricken jailbird, Harry Truman came back from Washington for the funeral. It was very bad publicity for Truman, but he said, "Pendergast was my friend and he was always fair with me."

Senator Truman

In 1934, Truman, who had handled the spending of millions of dollars without touching a thin dime, was having a hard time making ends meet on his small salary. His expenses had gone up and he was determined that his young daughter, Mary Margaret, should have the musical education her promising talent deserved. He asked Pendergast's permission to run for county assessor. But Boss Tom had promised the job to someone else. "The best I can do for you is senator."

"But I'd be worse off," Truman protested. "Five dollars a day while I'm at the capital."

"I mean United States senator," said Boss Tom.

Truman's enemies say that Pendergast boasted that he would show his power by making an office boy senator. This is a fabrication. The truth is that men of unquestioned integrity were scarce in the Pendergast machine and the Boss needed Harry Truman's unsullied record. In the witch hunt that followed the indictment of Pendergast in 1939, the eager investigators were unable to find a single doubtful action in Truman's record, though they tried their utmost.

When Truman filed in the primaries in 1934, every large newspaper in the state was against him. To his surprise, he won the nomination and was elected in November, 1934. He was very conscious of the honor of being a senator, and went to work to equip himself to deserve it. This was another period of growth, which

Truman, here as a Senator, always enjoyed a good laugh.

became apparent first in his work on the Senate Appropriations Committee, and then on the committee that bore his name.

When the war came in Europe, Truman became acutely conscious of the danger to America and of the inadequacy of her defenses. He decided to do something about it.

Complaints had come from Missouri that the construction of Fort Leonard Wood was being badly handled. In January, 1941, Truman went out to see for himself. He found waste, inefficiency, and disorganization rampant. Other camps that he visited were in a similar state. When he got back, Truman reported to the Senate, and proposed a committee to investigate the conduct of the defense effort while it was in progress—not afterward, when nothing could be done about it.

Grudgingly the Senate consented. The administration approved with even more misgivings, for they feared the disclosure of military secrets. Harry Truman was given the minute sum of $15,000 for his inquiry.

First he hand-picked his committee with an eye to getting hard workers. The counsel was the key position. Truman persuaded brilliant young Hugh Fulton to take the job by promising him that there would be no smearing, no whitewashing, no politics—nothing but the truth.

The Truman Committee

The Truman Committee made an outstanding contribution to the conduct of the war. No military secret leaked from them, though they knew all the vital statistics of war production. In addition to their investigations, they made such constructive moves as forcing the War Department to give Andrew Jackson Higgins a contract for landing craft, nudging the Navy into trying helicopters, and getting experiments started on rocket projectiles. Business men found they could trust Harry Truman's committee, and the Army and Navy admitted its value.

The day after Pearl Harbor, Truman got into his old uniform, went to the Secretary of War and asked for active service. Henry Stimson shook his head. "Senator, you are too valuable where you are."

The work of the Truman Committee was informed and guided by its chairman's philosophy of business, economics, and labor. He worked to preserve small business from being rubbed out by the rush of great industrial concerns. Even before D Day he was considering the best means of maintaining "a sound, healthy economy, capable of providing useful employment for all the facilities and labor which might not otherwise be fully utilized," in order that the home economy should not lose "the resiliency necessary for quick and successful conversion to peacetime occupations. . . . Our future must be based on an economy of plenty. . . ."

Vice-President Truman

The year 1944 saw Roosevelt's last and hardest battle for re-election. There was no question of his nomination; but the Vice-Presidency was the subject of violent controversy. Roosevelt favored Wallace. However, Democratic National Chairman Robert Hannegan told him that Wallace's unpopularity with the conservative Democrats might split the party. Senator James Byrnes was the strongest candidate, but the labor leaders were against him. Harry Truman was strongly favored. He did not want the nomination.

Two years ago the President told me the story of how he was persuaded to change his mind. He went to Chicago to nominate Jimmy Byrnes, and on Thursday night, after Roosevelt was nominated for the fourth time, he was still laboring to bring in delegates for Byrnes. Then Bob Hannegan sent for him.

"Harry," Bob said abruptly, "the Boss wants you to have it."

Truman's quick, impulsive reaction was negative. "In the first place, I don't believe you," he said, "and in the second place, I don't want it."

Bob Hannegan argued well into the night. Byrnes agreed to support Truman; the labor chieftains were for him. In the end he consented. Sitting at the big mahogany desk in the Executive Office, the President added, smiling rather ruefully, "and that is why I'm here."

In the late afternoon of April 12, 1945, Steve Early's voice sounded thick and strange over the telephone. "Come to the White House immediately," he said.

Truman did not dare ask why. He knew.

Two hours of confusion, and Truman found himself in the Cabinet Room of the White House. Bess was close to him, and Chief Justice Stone was standing in front of him. In his hand Truman held a little Bible that someone had handed him. The Chief Justice began to administer the Presidential oath. Truman could not speak for a moment, then he read the words from a slip of paper, ending with "So help me God." It was indeed a cry for help.

Truman The President

The hours of confusion became days. There was so much the President did not know; could never know. History was rushing like a wild, flooded river. Roosevelt's files were sealed and taken away, as is the invariable custom. His grieving advisers remained to help: Hopkins, wan and ghostly; the grim admirals, Leahy and King; General Marshall, who had wept as the new President took the oath; square-faced, steady Sam Rosenman; Steve Early, Jonathan Daniels, James Roosevelt, and Truman's own friend Jimmy Byrnes. They told him all they knew and showed him all the documents they had; but there were great gaps. He learned about the atom bomb—another awful decision to make.

The President felt very lost and lonely. He made many mistakes; but, as he said himself, "I don't look back and worry. If I did, I could never do the job."

Through all the confusion he was learning.

His purpose of doing what was right for Americans and for all people remained steadfast. And his ability to carry it out has enormously increased.

Because he is a man who forthrightly says what is on his mind, it is possible to know how President Truman stands on most questions of the day. His great preoccupation is with making a real, permanent peace. The "Truman Policy" is based on the belief of the President and his advisers that the way to world settlement is for us to be strong, and to use our strength to help those countries who choose to live in freedom. They feel that if the United States makes it clear just what it will fight for, there is less chance of our stumbling into war with Russia than if, by appeasing her with soft words and irresolute action, we lead her to assume, as Germany did, that we lack the will to defend the ideals by which we live.

Problems On Home Front

On the domestic front, the President seems less sure-footed. Part of his difficulty lies in the wide-open split in his own party between the ultra-conservative South, the wild and woolly West, and the radical vote in the industrial East. Also, a little of the New Deal's haziness on economics obscures his vision. His objectives of raising wages, supporting farm prices, and lowering the cost of living are mutually paradoxical.

As a poker player, the President frequently draws to an inside straight, for, as he says, "You can't win unless you take a chance like that." At times the inside-straight psychology seems to be applied in a wider field.

However, the President's domestic decisions are based on what he believes is right, without political fear or favor. When an issue leaves the realm of speculation and becomes plainly a matter of public interest, he does not hesitate to act swiftly and courageously—John L. Lewis will testify to that.

There is no longer any question that Truman will be the Democratic nominee to succeed himself. The Democratic National Committee is jubilant over his sky-rocketing in the public-opinion polls. And the 60 per cent of the people of the United States who believe that the President is doing a good job are right.

That famous headline; a moment Truman relished all his life.

117

The Truth About Dewey

by Alden Hatch

In 1947, talk about possible 1948 candidates was already in the air, and Alden Hatch assessed one GOP possibility.

Of all the gentlemen who yearn to be President of the United States, the shrewdest politician is Governor Thomas Edmund Dewey of New York. This statement is not intended as a slur. Given good will and high ideals, the expert technician is bound to do a better job of governing than an amateur.

Governor Dewey never does anything less than well. He has an absolute genius for organization, and he leaves nothing to chance. A more important political attribute is his ability to inspire devoted loyalty. Still another asset is the Governor's ability to keep his mouth shut.

Dewey's significant silences have given him a rather sphinxlike reputation. Many people simply cannot understand him. Part of the difficulty is geographical. With his well-tailored clothes, his sophisticated manner, and his cultivated voice, he seems to be a typical New Yorker.

But to understand the Governor it is necessary to take a look back at the little town of Owosso, Michigan, where in the early 1900s a man could live well on $1,800 a year, which Dewey's father did. Tom Dewey was born in an apartment over the general store owned by his maternal grandfather, Alfred Thomas. In a sense, he was born to politics, for his other grandfather, George Martin Dewey, was a founder of the Republican Party and the owner of two country newspapers. George Martin, Jr., Tom's father, edited one of the family papers, the *Owosso Times*.

Tom Dewey's dominant characteristics showed up early. "Honesty is the best policy" was the boy's guiding maxim. Eventually it became his trade-mark. Never has a politician been so aggressively incorruptible, or advertised the fact so well. The Dewey drive also appeared early. When he was 11, he got a job selling subscriptions to a magazine, and by the time he was 13 he had nine or ten boys working for him.

At 15, Dewey was too young to fight in World War I. So he took a summer job as a farm laborer, working from 5 A.M. until 8 P.M. He didn't like it, but he thus learned the farmer's problems by direct contact with the cussedness of cows, the wickedness of weeds, and the painful impact of the iron seat of a bumping reaper.

Music Vs. Law

In the fall of 1919, Dewey entered the University of Michigan with $800 he had saved. His grades were good but not gaudy. More important, he discovered that he had a spectacular baritone voice. Under the tutelage of William Wheeler, head of the music department, Dewey's singing won him first prize in the Michigan State contest and brought him a scholarship at the Chicago Musical College. There, the first girl he met, and the only one he could see, was Frances Eileen Hutt of Texas and Oklahoma, who was paying for her singing lessons by acting as Percy Rector Steven's secretary. The fact that she was returning to New York in the fall had a good deal to do with Dewey's decision to study law at Columbia University.

Dewey had taken law in his senior year at Michigan; though singing held far greater attractions, he wanted an alternate career. During his first years in New York it was a toss-up whether he would decide for the courtroom or the stage. However, he was quite sure that he wanted to marry Frances Hutt, whose sweet voice and silvery blonde beauty had won for her a singing role in George White's *Scandals*.

Dewey's final decision for jurisprduence was characteristic. He got a sore throat before an important concert and his mind promptly rejected a career that would be at the mercy of a microbe.

The next few years saw him pushing upward

through the crowd of aspiring young lawyers that clogged the courtrooms of New York. In June, 1928, when Dewey's salary was raised to $3,000 a year, he married his Frances. Among their best friends were the Elliott Bells. Young Bell was a financial reporter for the *Times*, and full of ideas and enthusiasm.

Dewey At Crossroads

Another friend, Sewell T. Tying, lured Dewey into the fold of the Young Republican Club, and set him to work ringing doorbells and exhorting housewives. The opposing Tammany braves were professionals, and, like many a successful general, Dewey got his education from the enemy.

Meanwhile Dewey was going up. In 1930 he earned $8,000 as an associate of the law firm of McNamara & Seymour. In December of that year, Destiny took him by the hand.

George Z. Medalie was engaged by the firm to try an important case, and Dewey went to see Medalie. Their meeting lasted from ten o'clock one morning until two the next. Medalie, dizzy with fatigue, recognized that he had encountered a young phenomenon. A few months later, Medalie was made U.S. Attorney for the Southern District of New York. He offered Dewey the post of Chief Assistant U.S. Attorney.

Tom Dewey was only 29. The offer was both a unique honor and a terrific challenge. It was also a crossroads abruptly reached with no advance warning. It meant giving up a lucrative income and a secure position. Frances was willing.

Dewey accepted the challenge.

To Tom Dewey, the condition of organized anarchy into which the era of bootlegging, gangsters, and rackets had thrown New York was intolerable. His war upon crime was to him a holy war, conducted in a spirit of pas-

Gov. and Mrs. Thomas Dewey open Dewey's Presidential campaign, 1948.

119

sionate righteousness.

Under the over-all guidance of Medalie, Dewey's aggressive campaign brought quick results. He set a record for convictions.

In 1933, Medalie resigned and Dewey opened his own law office. Clients came flocking and he made a great deal of money. So did the relieved racketeers. Then in 1935, Governor Herbert H. Lehman appointed Dewey special prosecutor to supplement efforts of New York's District Attorney, William C. Dodge. Yielding to the inevitable, Dodge gave Dewey a clear field as special rackets prosecutor.

Bounce Back From Defeat

This was Dewey's dream chance. He demanded and got his own setup—the fourteenth floor of the Woolworth Building and a staff of 20 assistants recruited from the most brilliant young lawyers in the city. At his word they followed him, leaving good salaries and secure jobs. They were the original "Dewey men."

As prosecuting attorney, Dewey was not a sympathetic figure. His principal handicaps have always been his demanding nature, his lack of heartiness, his very medium stature, and his brusqueness.

On the other hand, he was absolutely loyal

The Dewey's arrive in New York to await election returns.

to his subordinates, giving them a free hand and backing them up.

In August, 1937, Dewey agreed to run for District Attorney of New York County.

Dewey got a handsome plurality in the election and became a national figure. Then he suffered his first serious defeat.

The trail from a number of rackets led to James J. Hines, a boss of Tammany Hall—an untouchable. Dewey had been preparing a case against him for years. In May, 1938, Hines was arrested. The District Attorney came into court with an air-tight case; the evidence against Hines was damning. However, in cross-examining defense witness Lyon Boston, Dewey asked a question that might have incriminated Hines on charges other than those before the court. Lloyd Paul Stryker, defense counsel, leaped to his feet, demanding a mistrial. The courtroom boiled with confusion.

After two days' consideration, Justice Ferdinand Pecora ruled for a mistrial. Dewey went straight to his stricken staff.

"What will we do?" they asked.

Dewey smiled and said, "Move for a new trial. It will be the same indictment. We'll convict him."

They did.

Dewey bounced back from defeat right into the Republican nomination for Governor of New York in September, 1938. Governor Lehman beat him soundly. Dewey bounced back higher than ever.

Defeats And Victories

Early in January, 1939, Dewey found that he was leading in the polls for the Republican nomination for President in 1940. He asked Elliott Bell to help him form a group of advisers.

Bell came with him gladly, as did John Burton, who had a research bureau that he made available. Three other friends completed the group: Roger Straus of American Smelting and Refining; John Foster Dulles, an international lawyer who had been with Woodrow Wilson at Versailles; and George Z. Medalie.

Dewey came into the 1940 Republican National Convention with 360 delegates. Wendell Willkie had an unconsidered 107. However, Willkie's ardent idealism won him the nomination.

A tumultuous welcome greets Gov. and Mrs. Dewey in Los Angeles.

Dewey's four-year term as District Attorney ended on December 31, 1941. He went back into private practice, but he knew it would not be for long. It was, in fact, just eight months. Then the Republican Party nominated him for Governor of New York, and he was elected by a plurality of 647,628 votes.

In June 1944, the Republican National Convention nominated him virtually by acclamation.

Dewey's campaign was forceful and, in the main, on a high plane. But he fought under an impossible handicap. Wartime security made it difficult to attack the administration. Dewey could find out little about what was going on, and dared not use what he knew.

Dewey's defeat for the Presidency did not affect his popularity in New York. In the election of 1946 he was returned to office with a record-breaking 650,000 plurality.

An Ambitious Man

Governor Dewey has given New York an administration that is a marvel in this age of bureaucracies. This he has done, not alone by his dynamic ability, but by attracting to public service the highest type of men who in private life could earn ten times the salaries they are paid.

The Governor is an ambitious man, ruthlessly ambitious some think; but there is nothing mean or shortsighted about his method of attaining his goal. The only question he asks of a subordinate is, "Is this thing good for the people of the state?

My first sight of Governor Dewey was a pleasant shock. He was so much more vital than his pictures.

The Governor chatted wittily about everything under the sun, except the business at hand. Finally I dragged the conversation back to interview form by main strength, asking him bluntly what he thought of Vandenberg and his bi-partisan policy.

The Governor was for it. He said that he admired Vandenberg enormously. They had not always been friendly. "I don't think he liked being beaten in the primaries of 1940 by a little squirt," Dewey said with a grin, "but since then we have become great friends."

Then, speaking of the Truman-Vandenberg foreign policy, the Governor said very earnestly, "We must do everything in our power to counter the flow of Communism or we will be isolated. The pressure is no different from the Nazis, but it is run by smarter men."

I asked the Governor if he thought that the Russian system and ours could coexist in one world.

"I certainly think it's possible," he answered, "but only if we exist from strength—we must be as hard and as cunning as they—and only if we realize we cannot exist as a little island of freedom in a slave world."

I then asked the Governor questions about taxes, labor, depressions, finance, and the cost of living. He would not commit himself on any of these subjects, but I gathered that he was against sin.

I asked the Governor why he was willing to commit himself on our foreign policy and not about internal affairs. He answer solemnly, "Because that goes to the fundamentals of our national security."

We parted with real liking on both sides. I was quite aware that I had been given a run-around, but it was so beautifully done that I hardly minded. And I realized that it was very good politics.

There is no doubt of one thing: He is intensely anxious to be President. If nominated, he will put on the best-run campaign ever seen.

Dewey might make a splendid President. His administration would be miraculously efficient and he would streamline the inchoate federal agencies which have grown up planlessly under the pressure of necessity. He can claim to be one of the principal architects of the bi-partisan foreign policy, since it was he who sent John Foster Dulles to Cordell Hull in 1944; and he brought Dulles and Vandenberg together.

The Governor plays his cards close to his chest. Just at the end of our interview I said to him, "I'm going to ask you a question that I once asked President Truman."

Dewey braced himself.

"Do you ever draw to an inside straight?" I asked.

The Governor relaxed and laughed. "No," he said. "It's not a good bet."

"The President said that he often did," I remarked.

"That's not the way I play poker," said Governor Dewey.

It isn't the way he plays politics, either.

Dewey wins Republican nomination for Governor of New York, 1942.

The President and the General

In 1951, a former captain in the artillery fired one of the nation's top generals.

General Douglas MacArthur was a colorful figure, and a controversial one. When he returned to the United States from Korea in April 1951, he was accorded a hero's welcome. His triumphal parade in New York City drew more cheering spectators and more tons of torn up paper than had the homecoming of any previous hero. When he addressed Congress on Apirl 19, it was a moving emotional experience. One Representative was quoted as saying, "We heard God speak here today."

Yet this same General MacArthur who was being cheered and deified was a general who had just been relieved of his command and who had been accused only a few months earlier of having so underestimated a situation that his troops had had to make the most disastrous retreat in U.S. military history.

MacArthur and Truman: a clash of authority.

MacArthur's Third Major War

When the Communists invaded South Korea on June 25, 1950, MacArthur was quickly named Commander in Chief of the United Nations forces in Korea, then commander of the remnants of the South Korean troops, which were subsequently integrated with the U.N. troops.

Shortly after taking command, MacArthur announced that there would be no further retreating. The troops stood fast, then began the slow march northward toward the 38th Parallel, an arbitrary line which had been established when the Japanese were driven out at the end of World War II and the Russians put in charge of the portion of Korea to the north.

MacArthur wanted to push on through North Korea to the Yalu River, the boundary between

Korea and Manchuria. He met with President Truman on Wake Island in October and not long afterward received U.N. approval of the move. But his aims for an air offensive were frustrated by orders from Washington. His pilots were not allowed to destroy hydroelectric plants on the Yalu, nor the plants which furnished power to Manchuria and Siberia, nor the big supply depot at Racin in northeast Korea. And they were forbidden "hot pursuit" of enemy planes across the border. MacArthur's anger against his superiors began to grow.

The first hint that Chinese Communist forces might be in the field came in October, but it was late in November before they attacked in force. U.N. forces were sent reeling back. A new retreat began. In Washington the Joint Chiefs of Staff argued against making Korea the site of a major war, while MacArthur said that the fight for Korea was a fight against communism for Europe as well as for the Far East.

Views On Collision Course

The two viewpoints faced inevitable collision. MacArthur, an intelligent man, hated war; but he felt that the only way the suffering it brought about could be justified was to pursue it, once embarked upon, to the very end and final victory. "There is no substitute for victory," he was to say frequently.

On the other hand, the United Nations and President Truman wanted to contain communism in Korea, and they wanted to end the conflict "by peaceful means" and not risk a third world war. There could be no agreement between the two groups.

MacArthur pushed his views with vigor, and he was within his rights as a military commander to make his viewpoint known to his Commander in Chief, the President. However, he began making his viewpoint known to everyone. The principle of the supremacy of the civil authority over the military was at stake; by law the President is entitled to loyalty from his commanding officers, who either share his views or are willing to accommodate themselves to them.

Two statements by MacArthur precipitated the final confrontation. On March 24, 1951, without clearing it first with Washington, MacArthur issued a statement indicating his belief that Communist China was weak militarily and that the power of the U.S. and its allies might be used against the Chinese mainland. This was a challenge to the President's constitutional authority to make foreign policy; no soldier has that privilege.

Truman is believed to have made up his mind to relieve MacArthur upon reading that statement. But there was more to come. Representative Joseph Martin of Massachusetts, an isolationist, had written to MacArthur asking whether he agreed that Chinese Nationalist troops should be used in Korea. MacArthur's reply, which Martin read on the floor of the House on April 5, reiterated his belief that in order to preserve freedom the war in Korea must be won. Here again was a policy statement.

Truman's reaction was swift. He summoned his closest advisors and asked their opinions, although he had apparently already made up his mind. They agreed that the insubordination of the Far East commander posed a grave threat to the Administration. The Joint Chiefs of Staff also agreed.

Truman intended to have the notice of MacArthur's firing hand-delivered to him, but the *Chicago Tribune* got wind of the story first. When Truman learned that the paper was going to print the story, he released it to all the press. It was carried over the radio, and MacArthur learned the news from an aide who heard the broadcast.

The Hero Returns

MacArthur came home, and his homecoming was more like that of a conquering hero than a deposed general. His emotion charged speech before a joint session of Congress drew the largest radio and television audience ever recorded up to that time. There were many moist eyes as he closed with a reference to an old barracks ballad:

" 'Old soldiers never die, they just fade away.' And like the old soldier of that ballad, I now close my military career and just fade away—an old soldier who tried to do his duty as God gave him the light to see that duty. Goodbye."

The old soldier remained active in various civilian pursuits for thirteen more years. A full-scale Congressional hearing into the firing was launched. It did not clear up the conflicting issues, but it did show the American public that the Far Eastern situation was highly uncertain and the issues it bred were confused. In 1952, there was more talk of the Presidency, but MacArthur finally slammed shut the political door by accepting the position of Chairman of the Board of Remington Rand. He made speeches and was consulted by later Presidents, but the animosity between him and Truman never really ended. In April 1964 the old soldier died at Walter Reed Army Hospital in Washington.

The McCarthy Years

Senator Joseph R. McCarthy (R.-Wis.) was beginning to wonder whether he would be able to hold on to his job. The 1952 elections were two years away, but the junior senator from Wisconsin had accomplished relatively little so far in his first term in the United States Senate. What he needed was a dramatic issue, one that would make him known to the electorate. In communism he found that issue. He kept his Senate job, but as a result of his activities, scores of Americans, many of them innocent of wrongdoing, lost their own jobs.

A Timely Issue

Communism was a ready-made issue for Mc-Carthy. It was the era of the Cold War, the Hiss case, the defeat of Winston Churchill and his Conservative party in England, of Chiang Kai-shek's defeat at the hands of the Chinese Communists, of loyalty oaths, of security checks on teachers and other public employees, of spies and counterspies. The "Red Menace" had America worried.

After World War II, the former allies faced an ideological split. The Berlin Wall divided the West from the East; Russian coups in Hungary and Czechoslovakia intensified Western animosities and fears. When arrested in England as a spy, Klaus Fuchs, who had been at Los Alamos for the earliest tests of the atom bomb, implicated Americans David Greenglass, Harry Gold, and the Rosenbergs, among others, as part of a Soviet espionage ring. If these individuals had given the Russians top-secret U.S. information, people asked, what other traitors might be operating freely within our government?

The mood in the United States in the late forties and early fifties was a repressive one. Conservative groups, concerned with keeping America as it had once been, spoke out against communism and its threat to the nation. The more apprehensive citizens appointed themselves watchdogs of the nation. Anyone who might be a potential security risk was viewed with suspicion. Viewed with the most suspicion of all were those who had at any time in the past been associated with any Communist-front organization. Actually, many had joined in ignorance of the real purpose of such organizations and had been members for only a short time. Still, they automatically were painted as red, or at least pink.

Communist Hunt Not New

Joseph McCarthy was not the discoverer of the "Red Menace." The House Un-American Activities Committee had been operating since 1938, and history records previous attempts to ferret out security risks in government. But McCarthy, seeing the possibilities, exploited them to the fullest and reaped a bumper crop of publicity.

Regarded by many as a demagogue whose regard for truth was secondary to his ambition and whose capacity for stirring up mischief was limitless, McCarthy siezed on the times, and "McCarthyism" became to some a synonym for all that was bad in our government and to others a synonym for Americanism or patriotism.

McCarthy came from a poor family in Wisconsin. He listed 1909 as his birth date in the Congressional Directory, but records in his home township put it as 1908. He was the fifth of nine children in a pious Roman Catholic family. Considered somewhat unattractive as a child, he was said to have been especially favored by his mother, an Irish immigrant. His father, half-Irish and half-German, was a farmer. Before finishing high school, young Joe had worked as a chicken farmer and as a grocery clerk. He entered Marquette University

Senator Joseph R. McCarthy's anti-communist crusade during the 1950s ruined hundreds of lives.

to study engineering, but after two years changed to law.

McCarthy had been a small-town lawyer for a while, when at age twenty-eight he made an unsuccessful try for district attorney, running as a Democrat. Three years later he switched to the Republican Party and was elected a circuit judge. In his campaign literature, he tacked seven years to his opponent's age, saying the opponent was 73 (and on some occasions even 89) instead of 66, while subracting a year or two from his own age of 31. His campaign slogan was "Justice is Truth in Action."

McCarthy was a circuit judge for a little over four years. After the first two years, he applied for a commission in the Marine Corps and became a first lieutenant. His service was mostly in the Pacific—a desk job in intelligence. When in late 1944 the Marine Corps denied his request for a ninety-day leave so that he could go home to campaign for reelection as circuit judge, he resigned his commission. This was possible at the height of the war because as a judge he was exempt from military duty. He was reelected circuit judge and the next year

ran in the primaries for the Senate seat that had been held for twenty years by Robert M. La Follette, Jr., and for the twenty years before that by the senior La Follette, called by many one of the greatest U.S. Senators.

McCarthy's campaign was more aggressive than careful of facts. In his campaign literature, he claimed that he had enlisted in the Marine Corps as a private, that he had fought as a tail gunner in the Pacific, that he had been wounded, and that he had been on numerous combat missions, the number varying with the occasion. His slogan was "Congress Needs a Tail Gunner." In fact, he had not gone in as a private, no mention of combat missions appeared on his military record, he had sat in the tail gunner's seat as a passenger a few times on routine flights, and his "wound" was an injured foot sustained when he fell downstairs during a "shellback" initiation upon crossing the equator for the first time.

McCarthy's campaign tactics included, at one point, the implication that La Follette was a communist sympathizer, and at another, that his opponent had fascist leanings. After the

129

smoke cleared, McCarthy was the Republican candidate, and he was swept into the Senate on the wave that brought in a Republican-controlled Congress for the first time in sixteen years.

The First Shot

By 1950, after four years of doing nothing of particular note in the Congress of the United States, the freshman Senator from Wisconsin happened upon the issue that was to make him famous, or notorious. He fired his opening salvo on February 9. The occasion was a speech before a Women's Republican Club in Wheeling, West Virginia. McCarthy was not one to do extensive homework on a speech. He fell back upon a letter written in 1946 by President Harry S. Truman's Secretary of State, James F. Byrnes, who was replying to a query about security measures then in operation in the Department of State. The letter mentioned that of approximately 4,000 employees transferred into

the department from wartime agencies, a group of 284 had not been recommended for permanent employment, and 79 had already been separated from the service.

There was no firm evidence that those referred to in the letter were subversives, but McCarthy was off and running. He held aloft a paper and spoke:

> While I cannot take the time to name all of the men in the State Department who have been named as members of the Communist Party and members of a spy ring, I have here in my hand a list of 205 that were known to the Secretary of State as being members of the Communist Party and who nevertheless are still working and shaping the policy of the State Department.

Aside from the fact that this is his first known use of the often-repeated catch-phrase, "I have here in my hand a list . . .," the Wheeling speech set his pattern. Asked for the list by

"I have here in my hand..."; a familiar phrase to those who watched the hearings on television.

the State Department, McCarthy claimed he had said "205 bad security risks." A little later he changed it to "57 card-carrying Communists." At another time the figure was 81.

McCarthy had captured national attention. He had found his cause, and he made charge after charge, blackening names and reputations with a fine disregard of facts. He picked up many supporters along the way. Republicans, including Senator Robert A. Taft (R.-Ohio), were thinking ahead to the next election and the probable effect of McCarthy's crusade on Democratic chances. Sincere anti-Communists, extremists and malcontents, the China Lobby with its support of Chiang Kai-shek, those with private axes to grind, the Hearst newspapers, right-wing columnists such as Fulton Lewis Jr., and oil-rich Texans, joined his cause.

McCarthy employed a variety of tactics during his time in the spotlight. For example, he answered charges by counterattacking, obscured facts, put the burden of proof on the accused and on his listeners, and advanced the idea of guilt by association. He had his own intelligence source: people in government who let him have data from confidential files, either to curry favor or because they honestly believed in what he was doing. What they did violated federal regulations, and McCarthy knew it.

McCarthy nearly paralyzed two administrations as well as the Senate. The impenetrable clouds of smoke he set up had many voters believing that where there was smoke there probably was some fire. So their elected representatives did not dare speak too openly against the Wisconsin senator. A powerful object lesson was the unsuccessful bid for reelection of Senator Millard Tydings (D.-Md.).

The Tydings Committee

After the Wheeling speech, the Senate believed that McCarthy's charges were serious enough to warrant setting up a subcommittee to separate fact from fiction. Accordingly it set up what became known as the Tydings Committee, chaired by Millard Tydings, the conservative anti-New Deal Democrat who had first been elected to the Senate in 1926. The hearings opened March 8 and lasted four months. It was four months of confusion, tumult,

wrangling, and partisan politics. McCarthy named names, but never quite nailed down specific cases.

One example was Judge Dorothy Kenyon, a liberal lawyer from New York City, whom McCarthy accused, as one of those cited from the State Deaprtment, of being a member of "28 Communist-front organizations." As it turned out, Miss Kenyon was not even in the State Department, although she had served briefly on a United Nations Commission. Most of the twenty-eight organizations had not been cited as Communist-front, and in most cases Miss Kenyon's connection had been very brief or nonexistent.

McCarthy also charged that he had the name of Alger Hiss' superior, "the top Soviet agent in the U.S." This turned out to be Owen Lattimore, an expert on the Far East, consulted by but never employed by the State Department. A parade of witnesses was called, but nothing could be produced to support McCarthy's charges. Finally, J. Edgar Hoover, director of the F.B.I., testified that he personally had examined the security files on Lattimore and found nothing to indicate that Lattimore had ever been a Communist.

And so it went. McCarthy was unable to prove that any of those he had named from the State Department were guilty.

At the conclusion of the hearings, the Tydings Committee publicly rebuked McCarthy. Angered, the Wisconsin Senator looked for revenge. Helped by the publisher of the *Washington Times-Herald*, he put together a tabloid-type newspaper with a photograph of Tydings supposedly in conversation with Earl Browder. The caption read: "Communist leader Earl Browder, shown at left in this composite picture, was a star witness at the Tydings Committee hearings, and was cajoled into saying Owen Lattimore and others accused of disloyalty were not Communists. Tydings (right) answered, 'Oh, thank you, sir.' Browder testified in the best interests of the accused, naturally."

Half a million copies of the newspaper were distributed, and many readers failed to understand that the "composite" photograph referred to in the deliberately misleading caption was really a combination of other photographs, put together in the *Times-Herald* art department Eventually the whole story came out, but it was too late to keep Millard Tydings from losing the election. Other members of the Senate noted this lesson carefully.

Sound, Fury, and Targets

The McCarthy era, 1950-1954, was not a long period in American history, but it was "full of sound and fury." During the period between the Tydings Committee hearings and the Army-McCarthy hearings, Senator McCarthy, with the tacit support of some members of his party, lashed out at many targets. He kept demanding the resignation of Dean Acheson, the Secretary of State, and the impeachment of President Harry S. Truman.

When Mrs. Anna Rosenberg was nominated as Assistant Secretary of Defense, he fought to deny her Senate confirmation on the grounds that she had been and possibly still was a Communist. Mrs. Rosenberg, whose reputation and record for public service were both excellent, fought back. It turned out that an irresponsible informant had confused the Mrs. Rosenberg from New York with a woman of the same name on the West Coast. The latter had once twenty years before attended a meeting of a suspect organization. Mrs. Rosenberg was confirmed in the post.

Most disturbing to many people were his attacks on Secretary of Defense George C. Marshall, an outstanding soldier, former Chief of Staff, and former Secretary of State. Among the many charges he leveled at General Marshall were the following: he was "an instrument of the Soviet conspiracy," he was "a pathetic thing, completely unfit for high office," he had "an affinity for Chinese Reds."

The outbreak of the Korean War in 1950 strengthened McCarthy's position as it intensified the American public's already established fear of communism. A pall of apprehension and suspicion settled over the nation as blacklists and guilt by association seriously harmed many citizens.

At one time McCarthy charged President

Special Army Counsel Joseph Welsh calls McCarthy "reckless and cruel" during Army-McCarthy hearings.

Truman with starting the war for publicity purposes. When the President in 1951 relieved General Douglas MacArthur of his Far Eastern command, McCarthy was incensed. Asked for comment, he snapped, "The son of a bitch ought to be impeached."

While high administration officials and many of his own fellow-Senators trod warily lest they be tarred by McCarthy's brush, there were still those who spoke out. Margaret Chase Smith (R.-Me.) was one. She earned McCarthy's enmity with her "Declaration of Conscience," also signed by six other Republican Senators. She charged that the Senate had been "debased to the level of a forum of hate and character assassination sheltered by the shield of Congressional immunity."

Biggest Tactical Error

After the Republican sweep of 1952, McCarthy was made chairman of his own committee. As its chairman, he made what many believe was his greatest mistake. He hired as his chief counsel, Roy Cohn, 25, shrewd, aggressive, and arrogant. Cohn soon brought to the committee a close friend, G. David Schine, 26, an "unpaid consultant" on communism. Then McCarthy announced various investigations to be undertaken by his committee. One of them was to help put him on a collision course with the Army.

Charged with being a Communist was one Major Irving Peress, an Army dentist who had been honorably discharged for security reasons. Seeking the names of those who had let that "Fifth Amendment Communist" (a favorite term with McCarthy) be promoted and honorably discharged, McCarthy brutally castigated as "not fit to wear the uniform" his commanding officer, Brigadier General Ralph W. Zwicker, a much-decorated officer.

The climatic confrontation with the Army was precipitated by a reluctant private and his best friend. It was a confrontation watched avidly by some 20,000,000 television viewers, even beating out *I Love Lucy* in the ratings. G. David Schine, who had been classified 4-F, was reexamined, reclassified, and ordered to report for induction. Roy Cohn made extraordinary efforts to keep his friend out of the Army. When that failed, he tried to get a direct commission for Schine, whose life as a private with considerable preferential treatment was distinctly better than that of most Army inductees.

Meanwhile the McCarthy Committee had been investigating an alleged espionage plot at Fort Monmouth, the Army Signal Corps Radar Center. The threads of the various affairs (Peress, Fort Monmouth, Private Schine, and others) were finally brought together at the celebrated Army-McCarthy hearings, which opened April 22, 1954.

Senator Karl Mundt (R.-S.D.) was chairman of the committee. McCarthy, according to some, had intended to be witness, prosecutor, and judge, all in one, but he had to step down from the committee entirely for the duration of the proceedings.

At the hearings, the Army charged that McCarthy and Cohn had attempted to get preferential treatment for G. David Schine. On the other side, McCarthy, Cohn, and Francis Carr, the McCarthy Committee executive director, leveled forty-six charges, including one that the Army had tried to force them to halt their efforts to expose communist infiltration. Senator Mundt described the hearings as an attempt to separate truth from falsehood in the various charges.

The nation sat before their television sets for thirty-six days and watched McCarthy in action. It saw him use the device of "point of order" (usually a question of procedure or propriety) again and again to slow down or divert the hearings. It saw the badgering of witnesses and attacks on participants in the hearings, including members of the Committee itself. McCarthy's office had prepared, on all those involved in the hearings, dossiers which he used to throw on the defensive any who opposed him.

Joseph L. Welch, a courtly Boston lawyer, was the Army's special counsel. A skilled debater, he was a match for Cohn and the others. On the thirtieth day of the hearings, McCarthy raised another "point of order" at the end of a heated exchange between Welch and Roy Cohn. He charged that Frederick G. Fisher, a young member of Welch's Boston law firm, had been for some years a member of an organization named as "the legal bulwark of the Communist Party." At Harvard Law School young Fisher had belonged briefly to the National Lawyer's

Guild, which was now being charged with having Communist learnings. Fisher by then was a very respectable and conservative member of the law firm, and even Cohn had urged McCarthy not to bring up the matter.

McCarthy raised the issue, however, and in so doing brought about the end of the McCarthy era. Ignoring the warning looks from his supporters, he plunged on with his attack on the young lawyer. This was too much for Welch. He said, "Until this moment, Senator, I think I had never gauged your cruelty or your recklessness. . . . If it were in my power to forgive you for your reckless cruelty, I would do so. I like to think that I am a gentle man, but your forgiveness will have to come from someone other than me."

McCarthy, still unaware, blundered on, and a shocked, disillusioned nation watched. At the close of the debate, Welch walked out of the room amid prolonged applause. When McCarthy finally found someone who would talk to him, he spread his hands and asked helplessly and uncomprehendingly, "What did I do?"

The End Of The Era

The findings of the Committee were not particularly conclusive, but it was the political end of Senator Joseph R. McCarthy. Senator Ralph Flanders (R.-Vt.) introduced into the Senate a resolution of censure, and another committee was appointed, this time to take a look at the recently-concluded hearings as well as the other activities of the Wisconsin Senator. As a result, on December 22, 1954, the Senate voted 67 to 22 to "condemn" McCarthy, only the fourth Senator ever to be so rebuked by his fellows.

Joseph McCarthy remained in the Senate, but now he was out of the limelight. He continued to send to the White House insulting letters and telegrams which went unanswered. His speeches in the Senate had no impact, and the press, so influential in his rise, ignored him. By 1956, it was obvious that he was a sick man. On May 2, 1957, Senator Joseph R. McCarthy died of what was called an "acute hepatitic infection." But the McCarthy Era had died three years before, in June of 1954.

Journalist Edward R. Murrow exposed McCarthy on See It Now *television program.*

Ike

"Ike" Eisenhower was the nation's most popular military man. Either political party would have been happy to have him as its candidate.

No American in recent history so captured the respect, confidence, and affection of his countrymen as did Dwight D. Eisenhower. Other great men of his period, Franklin D. Roosevelt and Douglas MacArthur, for example, inspired extremes of feeling. But an overwhelming majority of Americans subscribed to the slogan, "I like Ike."

Virtually unknown at the beginning of World War II, he was, by 1945, one of the most esteemed of all Americans. From 1945 to 1948 he served as Chief of Staff. He told both parties he was unavailable for the Presidency in 1948. He became a president that year, but it was of Columbia University.

He served informally on the Joint Chiefs of Staff, meanwhile turning down numerous offers of lucrative positions in business and industry. Then came the Korean War, and President Truman, urged by the member nations, asked "Ike" to serve as Supreme Commander of the North Atlantic Treaty Organization.

Meanwhile, new pressures were building for Dwight Eisenhower to run for President, and in 1952 he retired from the Army to enter the political wars. Elected, he served two terms. In 1960, he retired to private life on his farm at Gettysburg, Pennsylvania. His army rank was restored by Congress.

Cadet Dwight David Eisenhower at West Point, 1915.

Lt. Eisenhower and wife, Mamie.

"Well, I'll be darned." Ike reacts to MacArthur's recall from Korea.

Eisenhower with Gen. Bernard Montgomery, England, 1944.

A talk in the field with Lt./Com. James J. Bradley, Fourth Army Deputy Chief of Staff.

Gen. Eisenhower swears in Gen. Omar N. Bradley as Army Chief of Staff.

President-elect Eisenhower with Henry Cabot Lodge, Jr.

Vice President-elect and Mrs. Richard M. Nixon.

Ike campaigns with New York Gov. Thomas Dewey (above) and celebrates election victory (right) with Mamie and

Ike and Mamie, 1959.

Ike pursues his favorite pastime.

Eisenhower takes oath of office as 33rd President of the U.S., 1957.

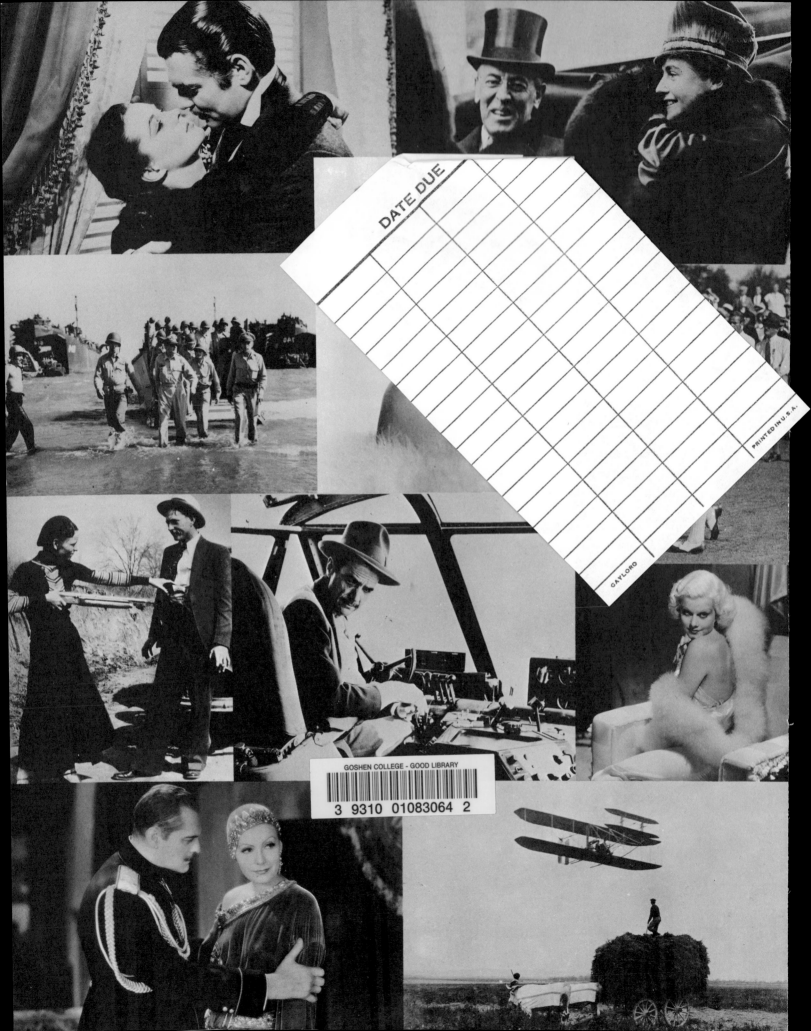